DEATH TRIP

A POST-HOLOCAUST PSYCHEDELIC MEMOIR

SETH LORINCZI

Spiral Path Collective

"In this deeply researched, beautifully written, and passionately
lived memoir of intergenerational trauma, Seth Lorinczi leads
the reader on a double journey: Into the harrowing bloodlands
of 20th-century fascism and, almost as scary, the miasmic
inner life of 21st-century, post-punk manhood. Brimming with
yearning, adventure, magic, and even comedy, *Death Trip*
stands as a testament to the power of writing to reshape reality
on the cellular level, and to the extremes we sometimes must
go in order to become sane. This is a good trip in the most
profound sense."

-Jon Raymond
Denial; Freebird; and others

"Seth Lorinczi's journey through MDMA therapy takes him into
a labyrinth of family secrets and ancestral trauma. The story
of what he finds there—and how it changes him—is as gripping
and propulsive as a crime novel. I was captivated the whole
way through."

-Leni Zumas
Red Clocks; The Listeners; Farewell, Navigator

"A very unique, courageous, and deeply moving book; I have
personally never seen anything else like it. A living exemplar of
the art of shamanic storytelling, of dreaming into experience
so as to live through and integrate unassimilated ancestral
trauma. In his honesty, vulnerability, and self-reflection he is a
way-shower, sharing with us his own one-of-a-kind encounter
with evil and his journey through our individual and collective
trauma in order to find the hidden treasure enfolded within the
darkness—our creative self. Bravo!"

-Paul Levy
Undreaming Wetiko; The Quantum Revelation; and others

"In this clear-eyed and tender investigation of family history,
intergenerational trauma, and the power of psychedelics to
help transcend the past, Lorinczi writes powerfully towards
forgiveness and healing."

-Rebecca Clarren
The Cost of Free Land; Kickdown

Please refer all pertinent questions to the publisher, Spiral Path Collective: www.spiralpathcollective.com

Published by Spiral Path Collective
6645 NE32nd Place
Portland, OR 97211

E-mail: pr@spiralpathcollective.com

www.spiralpathcollective.com

All photos are from the Lorinczi family archives, unless otherwise noted.

Cover art: Seth Lorinczi and Adriana Cordero
Book design: Adriana Cordero, designcordero.com

ISBN (print): 979-8-218-32023-2
ISBN (eBook): 979-8-218-32024-9

For my father; may it grant his soul some peace.

CONTENTS

FOREWORD

This is the part of the book in which I tell you that everything you're about to read is true, to the best of my recollection. And that's correct: I didn't invent anything that happens within these pages—even during the most whacked-out drug trip parts. Everything that happens actually happened, so far as I know—and I went to great lengths to try and verify everything I claim (and believe) to be true.

That said, there are exceptions. For one thing, there are the inevitable errors of memory, especially when attempting to recreate decades-old bits of dialogue. It's been said that every time we touch a memory we change it, and that each retelling only references the last version we told. Even those who, like myself, claim to have reasonably accurate recall often get things wrong, even when they're trying hard not to.

Then there are the conscious alterations. Some of the incidents I relate here occurred in a different order or timeframe than how I present them. In some instances, I did this to try and summon the sense of revelation and awe I felt as fragments of memory returned to me, or new answers to old questions were revealed, sometimes long after I'd forgotten I'd even asked them. Other times, I simply did it because I thought it made the story stronger. That's the storyteller's right, and I stand by it. I hope you won't hold it against me.

Speaking of stories, this one deserves a little introduction. More than anything, it's a tale of waking up to my own life after many years spent hiding from it. Even feeling, in my lowest moments, that I didn't deserve to live it.

The process of writing this book changed that. As I wrote it it was rewriting me, and I came to recognize that the alienation I'd always felt might have as much to do with my ancestors' life experiences as it did my own. I found this deeply liberating, and it opened many avenues of investigation. (In the very loosest sense, this is also the basic idea behind epigenetics; while this book certainly isn't scientific by any means, it's a topic you may find interesting in its own right.)

One more thing. It may sound counterintuitive, given that you're about to spend roughly a dozen hours reading about a stranger's life, but what I learned was that for all the pain in my family's backstory—the long and persistent threads of mass violence, antisemitism, and other forms of trauma—our story isn't actually all that remarkable. Go far back enough in time, and everyone's family story contains such wounds. Once I relinquished the conception of my family's story as being unusual, of our suffering somehow being more awful, noble, or historically significant than other people's, I found it freed me. I became less defensive and aggrieved, more generous and curious. More importantly—from your perspective at least—it made me a better storyteller. And it's a story I very much hope you enjoy.

Seth Lorinczi
Portland, August 2023

x

PART ONE

Freefall

My father and I, circa 1973

Prologue

Portland, September 2017: This is bad. Way worse than I thought it'd be.

Waves of nausea grip my guts. I'm sweating and my vision is crisscrossed by a sizzling grid of electricity. Everything looks shaky, as though my eyeballs were rattling in their sockets. But I'm immobile, pinned to the floor like an insect as the medicine burns through me like liquid phosphorous. This is some cosmic mistake, a sick joke, and I regret everything. Most of all following my wife's lead and saying *yes* to this demented clown show.

I'm in a suburban basement, splayed out on a rumpled nest of pillows and blankets. The air is thick with the scent of burning sage and a bracingly awful-smelling spray called *agua de florida*. Tacked-up tapestries cover the windows and doors, imparting all the mystique of a freshman dorm. Besides me and my wife, Julianna, the room contains two guides and twenty-odd other journeyers. Before an hour or so ago, I'd never met any of them. Now we're fellow travelers—or fellow inmates—each locked in our private struggles. Some writhe, moaning or crying softly. Others are silent and stiff as corpses.

And yet behind the chaos and the rank silliness there's something happening, something larger and somehow more real than anything I've ever experienced before. From somewhere very far away I sense the beat of a great heart pulsing through the ether. It is a sentience, or perhaps the sum of all sentiences, drawing me backwards in time, back through all the squandered hopes and false starts, the years I've spent watching my life pass by before me. It's bringing me back to some essential part of myself, a boy who learned too young that the world was not always a loving place.

Now the scene behind my eyes changes again. I'm floating down a river in a primitive dugout canoe. The sky is dark; scattered fires on the riverbanks cast a sickly light. In the flickers I see piles of rock and thatch, the rubble of villages. Maybe it's the end of the world. Maybe I'm no longer on Earth.

But I'm not alone. In the bottom of the rough-hewn hull lies a body: My father's. Even in the darkness, it's clear he's dead. His once-rounded form is withered and grey. Nauseating abscesses cover his skin: It's the cancer that killed him. Somehow it lives on, desperate for fuel.

I don't feel disgusted; I don't feel sad. I feel only a weary resignation as the canoe drifts ever farther down the fire-lit river. My father's been dead for twenty years and I'm still ferrying his corpse around.

1

Florida, March 1997: Grunting slightly as he braced himself against the bathroom wall, my father stood and waited for me to wipe his ass. Earlier that week, in obvious discomfort, he'd asked if I'd be willing to help clean him up, should the need arise. Now the need had arisen. The cancer had eaten through nerve and bone, reducing his excretory functions to the infantile state. As I wiped him down he spoke, so softly I could barely make out the words.

"If there were a million universes," he said, "each of them filled with spinning prayer wheels, it still wouldn't be enough to thank you."

That's a moment I'll savor for the rest of my life, both for its sweetness and its dissonance. *My father, talking about prayer wheels?* Honestly, he wouldn't have shocked me more if he'd told me he'd taken up pole dancing. Tender though it was, it was a reminder that even in this final chapter, my father could be as unknowable as the fog.

My father had come here to Florida to die. In his working days—and there were no days but—he was an attorney specializing in international trade. His short stature and absence of angularity only bolstered his professional image: A pleasingly cherubic face, full lips set in a half-smile, eyes bright underneath an artfully casual-looking combover. Each morning he'd shellack it into place, select one of his many tailored suits, and drive to his office a few blocks from K Street.

My father was a lifelong Francophile, and as such eating well was central to his self-image. As a result, my childhood was tainted by fear for his health. One could hardly have blamed his heart for simply throwing up its hands at the prospect of yet another filet mignon with *sauce béarnaise.* There were other consequences. His abbreviated stature—subject to interpretation, but 5 foot 6 on a good day—was hardly his fault, but it was exacerbated by a late-life adoption of tracksuits. This was an unfortunate choice, given his egg-like profile and aversion to actual exercise. But heart disease, as it turned out, was the least of his problems. Now—*surprise!*—cancer had come to stay. Hence Florida, and my new assignment as my father's chamber boy.

One afternoon, a few weeks before the end, I was startled by a wheezy call coming from my father's bedroom: "Seth! Stacey! Deborah!"

We hurried in from our various corners of the condo and found my father seated at the corner of his bed. His eyes were wide, as though he'd seen something that frightened him.

"I…I want you all to…to promise me," he said in a halting gasp.

We stood in a semicircle around him, waiting.

He gathered himself again. "I want you all to…to stay together," he managed. "After I'm gone."

Only the pathos of the moment stopped me from shooting Stacey a sideways glance. Who was he kidding? This last-ditch request was uncharacteristic, even bizarre. Whatever love bound the three of us together was streaked with merciless rivalry. I knew that once this was all over, we'd scatter to our respective corners. But I'll say this much: For a few weeks at least, we tried.

My sister Stacey and I began taking long walks on the beach, deriding the Floridians and their flawless tans. Mockery came easily to us; we'd navigated our turbulent childhoods through finely honed irony. But if Stacey looked up to me as her big brother she was also my competitor, fighting for the non-renewable resource of our father's love. By the time he'd relocated to Florida—the perfect setting for cancer!—Stacey and I had taken to cloaking all our interactions in sarcasm and black humor.

It was different with my cousin Deborah. Blunt and emotional, she's eighteen years older than me. And because she was more or less raised by my father and his first wife, she's more like a stepsister, if a distant one. I didn't see her much when I was growing up, maybe once or twice a year. But I loved her visits, and how they sent an otherwise lacking thrill of enthusiasm radiating through our hermetic household.

Not everyone felt this way. Invisible forces of attraction and repulsion seemed to draw my father and Deborah closer to and then farther from each other. I noticed how starchy and taut he'd become when she visited, slinking off to bed even earlier than usual. I just assumed my quiet and recessive father simply couldn't handle her emotionality. This was true, but not the whole truth. But I'm getting ahead of myself.

To be fair, Deborah's mood swings could set me on edge, too. But in the weeks following my father's uncharacteristic request, we tried to act more like family. After I'd swim my laps in the condo's otherwise abandoned pool, Deborah and I would soak in the adjoining hot tub. One evening as the last rays of sunlight cast their shadows over the plastic *chaises longues*, the talk turned to our family's lowest common denominator: food.

"It's weird," I said, "I never really cared about the food Grandma Csurka made. You know, the Hungarian stuff like stuffed cabbage. But I wish I knew how to cook it, now that...." I let the thought hang unsaid. *Now that my father's about to die.*

"Oh, Csurka was an incredible cook," said Deborah. "*Incredible!* On Sundays she'd spend all day cooking these insane feasts: Breaded cutlets—you know, *wienerschnitzel*—and this walnut layer cake called *dió torta*. But she wouldn't eat any of it herself."

"Why not?"

"Don't you remember her heart troubles? There was always this big fear she was gonna have another heart attack. So she'd make a bowl of green sugarless Jell-O and just kind of pick at it while everyone else ate."

I remembered my grandmother, of course: She moved in with us in 1975, after my grandfather Muki died. Csurka had more or less quit cooking by then, but once in a while my father could cajole her into making *rakott krumpli*, which sounds like a friendly dwarf but is really a deadly potato-and-egg casserole in a matrix of weaponized sour cream.

"Huh," I said. "The heart thing. It's funny how I grew up always thinking my dad was about to drop dead of a heart attack. I kind of forgot about his parents. That's what Muki died of, right?"

"Oh, yes. Just two months before your mom. Yup, 1975 was a bad, bad year." My skin grew prickly. I knew Deborah was trying to be sweet, in her way, but it was impossible to miss the faint whiff of superiority. That was the thing: Admit you knew less than her about anything and she'd hold it over you forever.

I was silent as the hot tub buffeted me with its super-chlorinated jets. Deborah's condescension was irksome, but it'd been years since I'd even thought about Csurka and Muki, and this bothered me. I realized I knew almost nothing about them: how they'd come to America, the stories of their lives back in Hungary. They'd always just been, well...*there*. Until they weren't. I could've asked Deborah to tell me more, but pride wouldn't let me. Now my father was preparing to wink out forever, and I had nearly no idea where we'd even come from.

Here's what I did know: I knew that my father was born in Hungary, in 1929. I knew that as Jews, my family occupied a complicated place in the nation's ethnic fabric. And I knew that at the close of World War II, they'd had to hide out somewhere. "It was a beautiful villa in the Buda Hills," my father told me, when I was about ten. "That's where we waited out the end of the war."

But what *had* happened there was a mystery. I knew that in late 1944, the Soviets came to liberate Hungary from German occupation. But my father wouldn't tell me much about it. Once, when I'd strewn the carpet of my boyhood room with LEGO bricks, he breezily remarked: "What happened in here? It looks like Budapest after the war!" I interpreted this to mean that, *sure*, things were messy for a while, but pretty soon they went back to normal.

My father arrived in the U.S. in 1948, after the Senate finally voted to allow large numbers of Jewish refugees in. My father took to Americanness with the zeal of a convert, speaking in an American English so neutral it was impossible to tell where he'd learned it (Michigan). And in response to the Jewish Question, my father adopted an ingenious stratagem: He stopped being Jewish.

Ignoring for a moment whether or not this was technically possible, the real issue was that he did a lousy job of it. Our world was a self-sustaining citadel of Hungarian Jewish refugees: Gerda Klay, my powder-scented piano teacher. Lola Varga, the anxious, frizzy-haired nanny who carted Stacey and me around in her objectively foul-smelling VW. And Doctor What's-his-name, the forbidding-looking dermatologist with the face of a war criminal. He'd been censured for treating acne with radiation years after it'd been recognized as harmful but *hey*, he was Hungarian, so he must be okay.

Most damning of all, my father was married three times in his life, each time to a Jewess. Still, no one ever once stated plainly: *We are Jews.* On Sundays my father dragged us to Unitarian church, where nobody seemed to worship much of anything. Our Judaism was more like a void, the screen burn lingering after the television was turned off.

So, what did I know? Nothing. By the time I got to Florida I'd more or less forgotten what little there was to be known of my family's backstory. This, of course, was according to my father's plan. I was meant to forget. But there was that single moment, a few days before the end, when I thought the door might finally crack open.

My father and I were sitting in the living room. It was evening time, the last shadows of day stealing across the carpet. Beyond the sliding glass door the Atlantic murmured and beckoned, but my father no longer seemed to care. Neither did I. I knew that soon he would end and the waves would continue. This thought became a Möbius strip, an abstraction looping in an endless stream.

My father turned and gestured for me to come near. As I knelt beside him, he spoke haltingly: "Do you…remember the movie…we watched?" A day or two before, we'd started *The Longest Day*, the 1962 D-Day flick starring John Wayne and seemingly every other male actor. The story held special resonance for my father. In June of 1944 Hungary had just been occupied by the Germans, their former allies. Everyone knew that the Soviet onslaught was far closer—and would be far uglier—than an American-led one. Still, the news from Normandy stoked the faintest embers of hope.

My father pressed on: "Do you…remember the scene. Where the Allied planes…fly over the beach. Over the German…antiaircraft guns?"

In an instant, every synapse snapped to attention. *This was it*, I was sure of it. This was the moment he'd finally spill the story, the moment all those dangling threads would suddenly knit themselves together. The room suddenly felt much smaller, a cave half-lit by torchlight. Humbled by this moment, one I'd longed for but never dared to expect, I drew even closer.

"Yes! I remember…. Tell me."

He croaked on: "The German gunners rushed out…."

I waited.

"The German gunners…." he paused for an eternity. "The German gunners…in the movie…."

My stomach clenched and unclenched itself like a fist. I didn't say a word.

"When they…ran outside." He gathered himself one last time. "Their…their belts…their belts were wrong. They should have had the equipment pouch on the…*right* side, not the left. That's where they kept their…entrenching tools."

Exhausted, he sank back into the couch's embrace.

"Huh," I said.

I would learn nothing more from him, at least not in the way I thought such things were learned. As suddenly as this portal had appeared, or appeared to have appeared, it was gone, and it would not show itself again. A couple of days later my father slipped into the fitful, days-long slumber preceding death, eventually dropping into a sleep so subterranean I had to strain to hear his exhalations. In the final minute of his life, his eyes suddenly snapped open—shockingly open, as if they'd never before seen—in an expression of surprise bordering on stark terror. Up, straight up, past his family gathered around him, up through the oatmeal-textured ceiling, through the placid Floridian sky, to whatever awaited him next.

Afterwards, for a single, holy hour, the condominium was held in a delicate spell. The body that had been my father's lay on the bed. Deborah and Stacey sat next to me. Besides our crying, which came and went in its waves, I detected the faintest of sounds: a silvery, shimmering tone. I thought back to the time when I was six or so, when I asked my father what the universe was.

"It's what surrounds our solar system," my father had said, adopting a familiar professorial tone.

"But...where does *it* end? What's outside of *it?*"

"No one can say, my darling. It's a container so vast that its boundaries cannot be known."

Finding this impossible to imagine, I'd turned back to my LEGO bricks. Now, in the dark of my Florida bedroom, I found it difficult to accept that with my father's passing, my conversation with him had also ended. What, then, would be my container? I got up and walked down the hall to my bedroom. Outside it was pitch dark, and with nothing to orient the eye, I imagined the apartment had somehow detached itself from its building. The Atlantic, invisible under an inky cloak, was silent. Perhaps it had dried up; it no longer mattered. I felt like a dust mote floating in the airless reaches of space.

I'd been here, or someplace like it, before. As a teenager, I'd gravitated hard to psychedelics. Wandering the moonlit alleyways of Washington, DC on LSD, I felt a keen sense of homecoming. If during the daytime I was anxious and insecure, here I felt a deep sense of belonging. Here's the thing: Psychedelics didn't warp my mind; they agreed with me, and I with them. Was that so wrong? But I'd left them behind years before, judging them unsuitable for a young person making his way in the world. In the process, I forgot nearly everything I'd been shown.

Now, in the floating apartment, I felt like I was tripping once again. The months of caring for my father had detached me from the world, and those nagging questions—*like, exactly what the hell I was doing with my life*—faded to a dull roar in the background. I found, much to my surprise, that I could navigate here. I was becoming no one, and I liked it. My only job was caring for my father, and I knew that I'd done it well. As I stood there in the darkened bedroom I felt a deep sense of wholeness and awe.

Then the doorbell rang. It was the undertakers: Two pimpled youths in cheap formalwear, barely bothering to conceal their smirks. They loaded my father's body onto a gurney and wheeled it away, never to be seen again. With that the spell broke. The silvery sound ceased, and the apartment sank back into its building with a silent settling of masonry and steel. The magic was over.

Deborah, Stacey, and I returned to Washington to attend to the funeral arrangements and the divvying up of my father's estate, and with this the bubble popped for good. As we squabbled over who'd keep the oil portrait of Uncle Desző and the modish Jensen silver, our fragile truce fell apart. The funeral complete, we went our separate ways and put the grief and the magic of our time in Florida behind us. Soon I'd forget nearly everything that had transpired there. The awe and wonder I'd felt, the sense of a greater purpose? They must have been figments of my imagination.

Just like that, with hardly a backwards glance, we let each other slip away.

2

Portland, July 2013: I nearly made it to my own wedding. Oh, I was there in body all right, bustling about as family and friends assembled in the sunlit backyard. But I also wasn't there, and no one was the wiser. Until it was time for us to say our vows. That's when it all began to fall apart.

We were to be married, Julianna and I, beneath the pergola. It was mid-July, the wooden slats already woven through with young grape leaves. The sun was brilliant but not yet scorching. Our yard—Julianna's pride and joy—was ablaze with sprays of native plants. Inside the house, platters overflowed with the foods I'd spent the last days preparing: Tunisian-style rockfish with harissa and rose petals, Lebanese-style lentils and rice, grilled lamb from a nearby ranch. Over a hundred people had gathered from all across the country to witness our union. I felt overcome by a thrill of anticipation, just like those last moments before I'd take the stage to play a rock show.

A few weeks before, Julianna and I sat down at the dining room table to discuss last-minute details. "I've been working on our vows," she said, "and I think you should say something too. Tell everyone what you're asking for, what you're calling in for this union. I want you say it not just to me, but to our friends. To our community."

Intoxicated by the hopefulness in her eyes, I felt a welcome glow suffusing me too. Marriage would be the bracing slap, erasing the lingering shadows of doubt. *This will change every-thing,* I thought. *We can do* anything *together!* "I love it," I said. The image of me addressing our friends ignited a flicker of pride. I resolved to begin composing my speech later, maybe after dinner.

Later, it'd seem like I'd only blinked and it was already the day of the ceremony. We'd gotten a permit to close off our block to traffic, which had the side benefit of distancing us from the black-painted school bus belonging to the polyamorous death cult down the street. We enlisted our six-year-old daughter, Evelyn, and her two cousins as flower girls. Now, as they walked up the gravel path tossing handfuls of petals behind them, a hush fell over the crowd. Julianna and I followed in their footsteps, our feet crunching softly on gravel. I held on to Julianna's arm tightly: A few days ago her knee had gone unexpectedly wob-bly, necessitating a last-minute set of thrift-store crutches. But for the moment at least, her legs were steady enough to get her to the altar.

We stood underneath the pergola, our guests' gazes resting easily on our faces. From the twitter of birdsong, the sweet promise of early-summer air, the sight of our two fluffy rabbits munching hay in their hutch, every sense was delighted. It felt like I was watching a movie of my life. And this time, for once, it had a happy ending.

A hush fell as the officiant—our former bandmate, Jen—stepped to the center of the patio. She faced the guests and began to read the preamble Julianna had spent the last weeks writing.

"Couples make pacts with one another all the time," she said. "whether they decide to marry or not. Some of these pacts are explicit. Some are unconscious. Sometimes we realize a pact we made years before doesn't work anymore, and no longer fits with the people we're changing into or aspiring to become.

"These realizations can make for real struggle, or they can make for transcendence. They don't need to explain us anymore.

They can provide cause to look at one another more deeply, and truly see. Or they can be reason enough to part."

As the warm sunshine beamed through the pergola I thought back to how hard the last years had been, harder than I'd believed possible. Between raising a young child and trying to make it as working musicians and artists, they'd nearly torn us apart. Incredibly, we'd made it here, to this perfect film version of a wedding. I reached out and squeezed Julianna's hand.

"I know you two," Jen went on, "and I know that in your years together there have been times when your partner has felt unknowable to you. Times when you have held on to one another across a great want. But you found that there was no person more suited to be your teacher and your healer than the person you marry today. And in a world that teaches us to armor ourselves, you found no one better to remove every piece of armor for, down to the last piece that covers your hearts."

A murmur of assent rose from the crowd. Now Jen turned to face me directly. "Seth, would you like to address your friends?"

With a silent *thunk*, the film stopped. The sprockets and gears seized, the acetate freezing in the searing light of the projector lamp. I'd completely forgotten to prepare something to say. Now our expectant guests' gaze felt like a wave of radiation. Prickles of sweat broke out all over my arms, and as panic enveloped me I shuffled between helpless excuses: *I thought it was just a suggestion! I didn't know we would be doing this now, in front of everyone! Can't this wait?* The film began to smolder and burn. A mocking voice whispered from somewhere deep inside me: *This was your only chance.*

We all stood there in silence—Julianna, Jen, myself, the people crammed into our backyard—for what felt like a very long time. Finally, I opened my mouth.

"I'm so…uh…grateful that you're all here. To see this. I love Julianna so much and I think…I mean, I *know*…that our lives will only be better for this," I stammered. "Um…thank you."

Everyone stood quietly, waiting for me to finish, or maybe to begin. If anyone noticed something amiss, they didn't say so. But as I turned towards Julianna, her eyes confirmed what I already knew: That I'd failed my one task.

We exchanged our rings. We said our vows. We kissed each other. But before I could duck out to check the food, Julianna caught my hand. "Baby, will you take a moment with me?" We walked to the back gate and slipped out into the alley behind our house. For all the activity and hubbub of the party it felt quiet and still here. Just us.

"What happened back there?" she said, her face betraying her pain. "I thought you were going to have something to say."

"I…I thought," I started, then stopped. What point was there? I looked in her eyes and saw the truth: I'd truly fucked it up. Somewhere deep inside my chest, tiny hands tore sheets of paper into little shreds. I looked past Julianna—*my wife*—down the alleyway. For a long moment I wondered if I should just start walking and never stop.

Something passed over and through us then. Whether some unseen hand or solar flare or a voice whispering through the ether, I'll never know. But something relinquished its hold, long enough at least for us to make it through this day.

"Come on," said Julianna. "Let's go back inside." We walked through the gate and back into the party.

The weirdest part was that no one knew. Everything was fine. By the time we'd reached the crowd lining up at the buffet table Julianna had recomposed herself, luminous under her tousled waves of hair and those bottomless blue eyes. She flashed that toothy grin and everyone cooed over her natural beauty and charm. I went down to the basement to grab my portable turntable and crates of vintage 45s, and soon the strains of The Music Machine, The Persuaders, and The Kinks drifted out over the neighborhood. I chatted with old friends and bandmates, Julianna's parents, my cousins from the East Coast. Later there was a singalong around the piano, a ridiculous mashup of old-school punk, '80s ballads, and musicals all swirled together. Hours later, Julianna and I dropped into bed, drained. She'd rallied and had a sweet, connective time after all. But when we awoke the next morning, something had changed. Julianna's face was pallid and drawn. She looked visibly unwell. Marrying me would nearly be the death of her.

3

Portland, August 2014: *I need this one. Please, don't fuck it up this time.*

Coffee mug clutched in one hand and laptop balanced in the other, I pulled open the door to my basement studio. Down here the air was cool and still, the only sound the faint hiss coming from the playback monitors. The room was dark, and as I took in the ghostly glow of vintage vacuum tubes and the whirr of ancient tape machines I felt comforted. My studio felt like a spaceship, and as I prepared to blast off I felt a special thrill: Today I had a mission to accomplish.

My job, such as it was, consisted of writing snippets of music for short films and commercials. It's how many musicians, even well-known ones, make a living between tours. The process is simple: A person called a "music supervisor" sends you a video and asks you to write a brief song to it, with specific parameters and in a specific style. Sometimes it's wholly original. More often it's a loose copy of an existing song the company can't afford. If the supervisor likes your work, your finished demo will compete against the other half-dozen to twenty composers all vying for the job. You get a couple of hundred bucks for submitting the demo. But if your piece is actually chosen, you'll make ten times that much, sometimes much more.

When I'd opened my laptop that morning and read the email, my heart gave a little leap:

> *From: Brett Doones*
> *To: 2-Track Seth*
> *Re: Stomper 4-Wheel Drive Spot*
> *Do you have time to pitch a demo? Here's the specs: Grimy garage rock. They want it to sound "punchy" and "upbeat." No vocals. Reference: The Black Keys. 60 seconds with a 30-second edit. Deadline: End of day. Demo fee $200.*

Never mind that I'd never listened to The Black Keys, or that writing a jingle to a car commercial felt slightly to majorly soul-defeating. I never turned down a single demo, no matter how out of my wheelhouse it might be. As a freelancer, I didn't feel like I had a lot of choice.

I loaded up the video so I could map out the beats. On the screen, fun-looking people did fun-looking things with a giant pickup truck. *Ugh.* Not the most inspiring material but *hey*, that was the job. At least the edits were easy to find; after scrolling through a couple of times, I saw the cuts lined up perfectly to a 4/4 beat. By the time I'd futzed with the map for another half hour, I'd established the rhythm well enough to lay down tracks.

Hoping the caffeine ripping through my veins might grant me a few moments of inspiration, I pulled open the heavy door to the soundproofed tracking room. Here the temperature was a few degrees chillier than the rest of the basement, the air more still and womblike. The walls were jammed with gear: Ancient tube amps, a hulking string bass, the wheezy reed organ I'd found in an alleyway. Most people wouldn't care that I used vintage gear to record demo tracks, but I knew better. Their inherent coolness would lend my demos a winning authenticity. Taken by their "realness" and "vibe," the producer would choose my track and I'd make a cool two grand for a single day's work. At least, that was the plan.

I plugged in my trusty old Guild electric and stationed myself in front of the video monitor. Now it was up to me. The trick was to write something catchy but not *too* catchy, memorable but not obtrusive. As the truck splashed through puddle after puddle I mirrored it with aggressive rock riffs, one after the other. But inspiration was a butterfly, bobbing just beyond my reach. None of what I was playing sounded the least bit interesting to me. After a couple of dozen tries, I sighed and sat down on the piano bench. The clock was ticking and with it a rising feeling of foreclosure: *Here it comes again.* Sooner or later I always came to this wall, the boundary of my aloneness. It'd be so much easier—*and a hell of a lot more fun*—if there were someone I could bounce ideas off of. But I wasn't really in a position to call in collaborators, not for a piddling $200 paycheck. At a loss for what else to play, I picked out a figure from one of the songs Julianna and I had written here in this rehearsal room, a few years before.

Music was our first connection. Julianna and I met in the Bay Area in the late '90s, when we were both drafted into a mutual friend's band. We moved to Portland in 2004, drawn by the promise of affordable home prices and a slower pace than San Francisco. We weren't exactly swimming in money, but the inheritance I'd received after my father's death was enough for us to buy a beautiful old Craftsman house, even take it easy for a while and not rush to get day jobs. We were going to indulge our creativity, give in to our untamed sides, make the art only we could make.

Now, of course, I see what a complicated gift the money was. How it provided a measure of safety, but also a place to hide when I least needed it. Imagining I had the talent and the connections to make it as a professional musician, I tried to shut out the quiet whisper of helplessness as our bank balance slowly dwindled.

Julianna—a far more natural artist than I—followed suit. A gifted painter, she sold a few prints here and there and waited for illustration jobs to fall into her lap. Whenever they did, I'd feel a thrill of relief. *See?* Now the money will start coming in, and we won't have to think about what we're doing with our lives.

But for all our cluelessness, one thing felt certain: When we made music together, everything felt okay. I knew we did something truly special, and it was just a matter of time before rest of the world caught on.

After we moved to Portland, we started a band: The Golden Bears. The name came to Julianna in a dream in which she'd been granted the greatest band name in history. Her startled laughter woke us both: "The Golden Bears?!?" she said, sitting up. "Um, that's *not* the greatest band name ever!" Still, how could we refuse it?

We'd recorded an album in 2006, when Julianna was pregnant. The day we got the test pressing, we lay down on the living room floor and played it over my ancient Grundig hifi. Though I'd heard the songs hundreds of times, I still found it hard to believe what we'd pulled off. The music was wild, beautiful, and strange: A mashup of vivid psychedelia and '60s pop, worshipful folk and unhinged freakouts. It sounded like nothing else, a testament to our promise and a hymn to our forthcoming child. When the final song was done, Julianna turned to me, her face wet with tears. "Baby," she said. "I want us to become the people who made that record." The following spring, after our daughter Evelyn was born, we scraped together a live band with friends and began playing out. One night, after a handful of under-attended shows, it all clicked into place.

It was at The Doug Fir, a log-walled nightclub with good sound and a rustic-chic vibe. I knew the place would be packed: We were opening for Quasi, a near-legendary fixture in the Portland scene. The plan was that after soundcheck, Julianna would zip home to put Evelyn to bed, then a sitter would arrive to take over. As the first show goers filtered in I snuck anxious glances at the door, hoping against hope the room would be at least half-full by the time our set began.

Then I got the text from Julianna. "Kid's not going to sleep! I'll do my best to be on time. Stall!"

"Okay, but hurry!" I wrote back, my jaw tightening.

I'd known that trying to play a rock show with an infant at home was rolling the dice, but my stomach gave a little flip anyway. Our set had to end at 9:15 sharp, and because Julianna was both the singer and the drummer, starting without her wasn't really an option. My nerves jangling, I made my way backstage. As I tuned and retuned my Guild, a staffer in a Doug Fir t-shirt appeared at the door of the green room. "Okay Golden Bears!" he said. "Five minutes till set time!"

"Uh, no problem!" I replied. "Ready to go!"

I glanced at my phone. "HURRY!" I texted. By the time Julianna finally burst through the door, ten minutes later, Doug Fir guy was glaring bullets at me. "Okay, I'm here!" Julianna panted. "Everything's going to be fine! Jesus I have to pee!"

A minute later we took the stage to an expectant hush. To my relief, the room was full, and I saw the faces of a few friends scattered among the crowd. But Julianna didn't sit down behind her drum kit. Instead, she stepped to the front of the stage and grabbed the microphone off its stand.

"Hey everyone, sorry I was a little late!" she said with a self-deprecating laugh. "Seth and I have a new baby at home and…it's really awkward tucking her in and trying to juggle these two worlds.

"As I was driving here, I was thinking about what's happening far away in Palestine right now. I saw this footage this morning of a woman cowering with her baby while missiles rained down. Can you imagine?"

I heard a murmur coming from the crowd, a shouted: *"Fuck no!"* The news had been particularly grim that month: The Israel-Palestine conflict had flared up again, and many of our friends felt agonized and hopeless. *Still, where was she going with this?*

"I'm singing tonight for those mamas and their babies, and for this bewildered world that I love so much. I'm so happy to be here!"

The room erupted in cheers. As she stepped back to her kit I caught Julianna's eye and mouthed an appreciative "Wow!" She beamed a smile back at me, and her love for me was a volcano inside my chest. The whole room knew it. My nervousness from a few minutes before had evaporated; now I felt like I was about to be shot out of a cannon.

I was. As we launched into "Tall Ships," the first song on our record, I felt the power of what we'd done. A simple and insistent pulse built into a soaring slab of psych-rock and suddenly we were aloft. The sound was perfect, my guitar a flamethrower. When I dared to snatch glimpses of the faces in the crowd, I could see it happening in real time: Our music was cracking them open, expressions of naked wonder breaking through the Portland remove. After a caustic guitar break the song suddenly downshifted into an eerie ballad, the music as hushed and sepulchral as it had been scorching a moment before. Save for Julianna's luminous voice and a ghostly drone of feedback, there was only the sound of three hundred people holding their breath.

The next forty-five minutes rolled out in a blur, no breaks and no stops. I seemed to float a few inches above the stage, my hands tracking every inflection of Julianna's as they put her battered Slingerland kit through its paces. This was our communion, our lovemaking, and tonight it was a wellspring of fire. By the end of the set I was breathless with elation, and I knew that nothing stood in our way.

But then it changed.

That night as we gathered backstage after our set, something felt off. While I quaffed beers and joked with our bandmates Julianna was barely verbal, lost in some interior cavern.

"You okay?" I asked her later as we loaded up our battered minivan. Her eyes looked haunted.

"Yeah. It's just...it's hard to switch back from giving so much away. From feeling so naked."

I didn't say anything. I figured it would pass, that she'd get over it. This was what we were working towards, wasn't it? To be seen, to be acknowledged, to be recognized? I knew she'd come to her senses.

Over the coming months, I felt the slightest of buzzes coalescing around our band. Nothing much, just a couple of mentions in the local press, a few more opening slots. But it sent my tendency towards rigidness and control into overdrive. Even if the record we'd made was deeply personal and blessedly uncommercial, I insisted that Julianna and I make it our job.

"Look, we have to take this seriously," I said during rehearsal one day. "We need to tour. And I need better gear so we can make better-sounding records."

"I don't know about this, baby. Maybe there's another way to do it. Do we really want to go out on the road?"

"How else are we going to sell the record? These are the realities of being in a band. It takes hard work. We need to try harder, that's all."

It worked, almost. We made a second record. A good one, if it lacked the magic of the first. But because it was released on a more proper label than the previous album, both iTunes and Amazon Music made it their front-page picks. Finally, we were on our way! All of the years spent learning the craft and playing shit shows to nobody were finally going to pay off. The world had come around, just like I always knew it would.

But then nothing happened.

I mean that literally: nothing. Outside our circle of friends, no one bought the album. To make matters worse, I'd booked us a weeklong residency at a downtown nightclub. Surely the opportunity to see a band of rising stars in this intimate environment would draw in droves of new fans. We'd stretch out a bit, invite special guests, learn some fun covers. *They'll see we're artists, not just another rock band!*

You see where this is heading, don't you?

It's one thing to play a show to nobody. You suck it up, get a little tipsy, laugh with your bandmates, make a joke out of it. It's another thing to do it night after night after night. Each evening, Julianna and I wearily greeted the babysitter and drove downtown to our execution. It didn't matter that our songs were tightly constructed gems, or that we'd chosen clever cover songs to please die-hard obscuro music fans. It didn't even matter that Julianna was a luminous and soulful singer who was drumming like a demon through the pain in her guts, the pain we'd soon learn was an autoimmune disorder run rampant. Glaring out at the near-empty room, I felt hot shame dripping through me. I thought we'd done everything right, but it'd come out all wrong.

Driving home after the final night, wedged beneath a snare drum and a box of unsold records, Julianna finally broke open. "I can't do this," she sobbed, the tears finally spilling forth. "I can't go on feeling like a loser."

And just like that, it all fell apart. She quit our band. With our first language of intimacy stripped away, we were left with just ourselves, our three-year-old daughter, and a house that always felt slightly too big and too cold.

I blinked and startled myself back to the present. That was four years ago. Now it was 2014, and I had a demo to finish. There was no point in reliving the past. Those quiet strums had unleashed a flood of feelings I didn't want to feel. I put my guitar back down and went upstairs to brew an emergency round of coffee.

Julianna came in from her studio in the corner bedroom. "Hey," she said. Her face was taut. "Um…how much longer you going to be working on that thing? It's pretty loud up here."

"Until it's finished," I said, more sharply than I'd planned. "I'm sorry," I quickly added. "I'm trying to get it done but…I just feel like I can't grasp it." I heard the pleading tone in my voice and inwardly winced.

"I'm so sorry. Maybe you can give it a rest? It sounds like you're trying to force it."

"I don't really have a choice," I snapped. "I have to turn it in today. I'll get it soon, I'm sure." I watched as Julianna's expression tightened, felt the familiar confirmation of my pettiness. But what else could I do? She just didn't understand that a job was a job. For the briefest flicker, I knew that what I wanted was for her to take care of it, to remove the cloak of failure that dogged me. But that only sent another wave of shame rippling through me.

After another half hour of noodling I settled on one of the canned rock riffs I'd played earlier. I overdubbed some percussion to make it sound "live" and "real" (but not too "live" or "real"). I mixed it, uploaded the file, and wrote the music supervisor back. But before I'd even hit "send," I knew this demo—like all of them—wasn't going to get picked. *At least I made a few bucks,* I thought, anticipating the couple of glasses of wine I felt I'd earned. *Any day now, I'll break through.*

4

Portland, November 2015: I pulled into the gravel lot, steering carefully through a minefield of ominous-looking puddles. *Not exactly Portland's most promising location, but just about right for this crowd.* A hand-drawn sign in the window read "Red Devil Film Production." I took a deep breath and steadied myself. *I need this. Please...don't blow it.*

Behind the creaky metal door was a cramped and chaotic office space. The floor was a jumble of desks, filing cabinets, and lockers overflowing with cameras and gear. "Hey Nancy," I called out to the young woman hunched behind one of the desks. "How you doing?"

"Seth, nice to see you. Busy! I fly out to Panama tomorrow."

"Oh, how cool! Watch out for snakes!"

Nancy was a producer at Red Devil. Like her, the company was always on the go, hustling new projects and scooping up awards for its short films. "Ron's in the editing suite," she said. "You can go right in."

I picked my way through a thicket of tripods to a grey-walled room in the back of the building. Ron Wilson, Red Devil's creative director, sat hunched before a giant flat-screen monitor. "Hey Seth!" he called over his shoulder. "Give me just a minute."

I plopped down on the couch at the back wall and waited. Visiting the office both thrilled me and fired my latent anxiety in equal measures. I didn't really need to be here; going over a creative brief could just as easily be done over phone or email. But I always came to the office because I thought it would somehow make me seem more like part of the team. More essential.

Ron turned from his desk. A slight man with an impish cast, I'd pegged him as the source of Red Devil's soulfulness. "Hey, sorry to make you wait, and thanks for coming down. You read the email, so you know what this is about, right?"

"Yeah, the family who spends a year traveling in memory of their mom."

"Right. It's such a beautiful story, how the daughters overcome their anxieties after she dies."

"Well, the brief really touched me. My mother died when I was four, so it feels kind of personal."

Something flickered over Ron's expression. "It wasn't actually that big of a deal," I said, wishing I'd kept my mouth shut. "We got through it."

"Well, let me walk you through the scenes." He turned back to the monitor and began scrolling through the video.

By the time I left, a quarter of an hour later, I was feeling all right. This time I'd write a score so poignant and evocative that the higher-ups at Red Devil would have no choice but to take me on as their in-house composer. I'd play coy at first, claiming the freelance life suited me better, before finally capitulating and joining the team.

I let the feeling of promise percolate through me as I drove home through the Portland drizzle. Back in my basement studio, I loaded up the video Ron had given me and began laying out the cuts. On-screen, the father and his two young daughters stride through an airport. The mother has just died from cancer at the age of 48. But she's very much alive as the scene shifts to flashback: Here's the entire family posing against a grab bag of exotic sites: Roman ruins, the Great Pyramids, the Golden Gate bridge. The daughters wear expressions of naked delight as they cavort in a forest pool somewhere in Southeast Asia, flanked by a pair of elephants. They've determined they'll go everywhere, experience everything, seize every drop of life even as their mother drains away week by week. As the film depicts the daughters' final hugs with their mother—hairless and spent in a wheelchair—the father finally breaks down.

That's when I broke down, too. Alone in my spaceship of a studio with no witness but the twinkling lights and silent dials, my body betrayed me. The tears gushed forth, and there was nothing I could do to stop them. The family on the screen were living out their wildest dreams, their lives expanded despite their tragedy. Me? I'd never really done anything. Right now I wanted to *be* that other father: the grief-stricken widower, plucky and admirable. I imagined myself in his place, heartbroken but stoic. Eventually someone new would come into my life and care for me, someone who wouldn't demand too much of me, given everything I'd been through. Then I'd belong to something, even if it were only the brotherhood of lost men.

I didn't go upstairs to Julianna and tell her that I wanted to live my life differently. I didn't go find Evelyn, hold her in my arms and remind her how precious she was to me. Instead, just like that, the brief chasm that had opened inside closed back up again. I wiped my eyes and focused on the job.

By the time I'd finished a rough draft, the light outside was fading. As I played back the film, I didn't feel raw any more. The images of heartbreak and wonder were just edit points, and the music I'd written sounded like everything else I did: Brief flashes of inspiration, the rest of it wallpaper. *Why was this so hard?* I craved the solace of dinner and the wine that would entail. *At least I had a job today*, I thought. *I ought to be grateful.*

Later that night, after we'd put Evelyn to bed, Julianna and I met in our bedroom. We'd been tossing around the idea of a financial meeting for weeks though somehow, it always seemed to get postponed. I felt a familiar apprehension stirring in the pit of my belly as I sat down at the foot of the bed.

"How was your day?" said Julianna.

"Eh, not great. I made some progress on this film but it doesn't sound great. I can feel myself grinding."

"I'm sorry to hear that," she said. "You'll figure it out."

"What about you? What's going on with your work?" I said, following a familiar line of questioning. "Why don't you try to find more illustration jobs? That deck turned out so well!" A few years before, Julianna was hired to illustrate a set of tarot cards. It was a great gig for a major publisher. But since then, she'd never advertised herself as a hired gun.

"I'm still working on that commission," said Julianna, "and another's coming in next month. But it's hard to focus on anything when I feel so awful all the time. I got some results back from the naturopath and it looks like the best thing to do is to follow this stupid diet where I can only eat like three things. I don't know how I'm going to put on any weight just eating squash and bone broth."

"I know, I know. I'm sorry. But…I really wish you'd do something with all your talent."

Julianna's paintings were tiny jewel boxes, imaginative and precise. And when she sang or drummed, it was like she went into channel, deep into some spirit realm to which I lacked access. But outside of that, she seemed incapable of sharing her gifts. She'd resort to shyness and self-deprecation, sometimes even covering her mouth when she spoke. Her reluctance to promote herself was maddening, given the depth of her talents.

"Look, my body's in real trouble," she said. "And you act like we're going to be evicted tomorrow. That's not what's happening. You seem so afraid all the time. There's no wolf at the door; we're safe. And I need to get better. I need to get better and I'm going to get better, but not with you pacing this house like you're about to walk the plank!"

We stared at each other.

"Look, the doctor also gave me a recommendation to work with this shamanic healer," she went on. "It's pretty far out but I'm hopeful and a little desperate."

At this I finally boiled over. "We've got *nothing!*" I said, louder than I'd intended. "The roof is falling in and we don't know what the fuck we're doing. Why do you want to talk to a *shaman?*"

Julianna got up and stormed downstairs.

For a single flaming moment, I considered hurling our bedroom furniture—or myself—through the window. Why did this feel so wrong? Marriage was supposed to be the finish line. Or maybe it was the opposite: the ultimate admission of defeat, the caving in to inevitability. Either way, it didn't really matter. Why we were doing this to ourselves? After a moment I followed Julianna downstairs.

I found her sitting on the kitchen floor, her head resting on her knees. She was feeling around as if she were blind, touching the faces of the built-in cabinets, the wooden planking of the floor. I found it unsettling and I glared at her, toggling between anger and fright.

"I know this is all so fucking *real,*" she said. "I know this is so *important,* that we have to do all the *things,* we have to be good *parents* and make *money* and think about our *retirement.* But sometimes I just want to meet you outside of the story. I want to pop our heads above the big fucking story and just *be* for a minute."

I fixed her with a look of utter contempt: "You say this shit to me and I don't understand what you're even talking about." At this Julianna curled on her side and began to wail like an animal. I left and went downstairs to the basement.

I looked around in the cool silence. Everything seemed so right: The gleaming metal of old preamps, the Art Deco knobs of vintage equalizers. My studio was my crowning achievement, a perfect time capsule. So why didn't it give me any comfort? And why couldn't I seem to create anything meaningful here? I wondered how long Julianna and I would go without speaking this time around, how we'd manage to disguise the icy silence around our daughter. For a moment, a snippet of lyrics Julianna had written for our now-defunct band flashed through me:

> *From my tree bough I saw you*
> *Saw my shadow cast upon your floor*
> *So tell me lover, tell me lover do*
> *What does your window part us for?*

I'd heard them hundreds of times, but I'd never really bothered to listen. I wonder now how much easier everything could have been if I had.

5

Portland, May 2016: It wasn't Julianna's autoimmune disorder that woke me up, or my latent depression. What finally shook me awake was the death of a rabbit.

We'd gotten the matching pair of rabbits after Evelyn's preschool teacher asked for help housing the larger number of rabbits that results from a smaller number of rabbits. Fruitcake and Nutcake came to live with us and brought a disproportionate degree of delight, given their placid demeanors and resolutely expressionless faces. They made us seem more playful and freewheeling than we actually were. *Look at us!* I marveled. *See? We are having fun!*

But if in theory the rabbits were Evelyn's, it soon became clear that I held the greatest emotional stake in their well-being. During the daytime they had free range in the yard, and at night I'd lie awake worrying about the dogs, hawks, and other predators who patrolled the neighborhood, not to mention the potentially toxic plants. I didn't see my anxiety as a problem. *This was merely the price of loving something*, I reasoned, and the spikes of dread coursing through me were simply proof of my devotion.

All was well, until it wasn't. One afternoon, three years after we'd taken on the rabbits, I saw a still white shape by their hutch. It was Fruitcake—the goofier, more blobular one—and he seemed barely alive. It happened to be Julianna's birthday, and we were supposed to drive to her mother's house for a celebratory dinner. "Jesus," Julianna fumed as I dithered and wrung my hands by the rabbit hutch. "Can we please leave already? The fucking rabbit can wait."

"I…but…he's clearly sick," I choked out. "We can't just leave him here, can we?" Eventually, I persuaded her to detour for a costly vet visit. An hour and a half later we arrived at her mother's house with the sick rabbit in a cardboard box. A few days later, we laid Fruitcake's lifeless body on a cloth shroud surrounded by flowers; then I dug a hole in the backyard and we gently lowered him inside.

It wasn't the first time we'd lost a pet, but this time something was different. It was the first time Evelyn had experienced death so closely, and her shock and sadness touched a deeply buried nerve in me. But as she metabolized the loss in the coming days, it wasn't her that needed consoling: It was me. Grief was a stunning slap across my face, and I felt myself slipping into waters of an unknown depth. In the weeks to come the sadness refused to subside; I'd break down sobbing in inopportune locations, like the locker room of the local community center. My reaction felt disproportionate, even unseemly—*it's just a rabbit!*—and yet I couldn't break free. Fruitcake had been under my protection and I'd failed him.

The weirdest part? Despite the discomfort, some part of me actually liked it here. In these unfamiliar borderlands the hours seemed to warble and sway, melting into one another like mesmerizing drops of mercury. Reminded of that precious hour after my father had passed, I felt a simple awe. It'd been years since I'd realized it was possible to feel this much.

A couple of weeks later, Julianna returned from an errand. Her face was lit up: "Have you heard of Rachel Yehuda? I just heard her interviewed on the radio. She was talking about something called 'epigenetics.' And she's done a bunch of research on the children of Holocaust survivors. You should really check it out!"

"Huh. Okay."

It took me a few days, but eventually I listened to the interview. As Dr. Yehuda explained the basic idea behind epigenetics—that our ancestors' life experiences can impact the way our genes function—I felt something stirring. I hadn't really given much thought to my predecessors and their life experiences. Now, hearing how children *in utero* during wartime or other external stressors were more likely to develop heart disease, obesity, even schizophrenia, I sensed a circuit board inside my chest, a neat grid of wires and resistors. What if some shadow program had been running this whole time without my even knowing it?

Epigenetics is still an emerging science, cautioned Dr. Yehuda. One counterargument is that the anxiety the offspring of survivors feel is merely the result of the traumatizing stories they've grown up around. But I hadn't really been told any stories, more like *stories* of stories. The walls of my childhood home were lined with thousands of books, many of them about the experience of trauma, dislocation, and war: *The War Against the Jews, The Wehrmacht, A Bridge Too Far*. But amongst all these stories of tragedy and loss, one was nowhere to be found: Our own. No one told me what'd happened to my father's extended family, to the aunts and uncles and cousins and great-grandparents whose names I didn't even know. As Dr. Yehuda went on about how children of Holocaust survivors tend to experience a heightened stress response and higher rates of anxiety and depression, I felt like I'd fallen through some trapdoor inside myself, one I'd walked by all these years but never bothered to examine. Now

I stood inside some darkened internal room, surrounded by murmuring voices. Whose were they?

In the days to come, Dr. Yehuda's words continued to echo and ping inside me, setting off one tiny aftershock after another. Maybe I had more of a backstory than I'd realized, but… how would I even begin to learn about it? I could call Deborah, but we hadn't really been on speaking terms since my father's death. Stacey? She had no interest in our family history. Then it came to me, and I nearly smacked my head in disbelief. *Dummy!* I walked upstairs to the little closet off our bedroom and opened the filing cabinet in the corner. There it was, tucked in the back: A manila folder stuffed with yellowing typewriter stock. My father's memoirs.

Maybe "memoirs" is the wrong word. They're more like Cliff Notes: twenty-five typewritten pages, give or take. For a man so devoted to record-keeping, it'd been strangely difficult to get him to write them at all. Now, as I drew out the crinkled pages, I was grateful I'd persisted. Some part of me must have known that one day I'd need them.

It had been twenty years since I'd even looked at them, and the mere sight of the font—Courier 12, embossed from the floating silver ball on my father's Selectric—touched something in me. I missed my father more than ever, and as I began to read he suddenly seemed quite close, a presence hovering just above my shoulder. As his precise constructions brought him back to life I was filled with a quiet sense of awe. Right here, on these yellowing pages, was a map of my family's ley lines:

> *You have, to my great pleasure, expressed an interest*
> *in my recollections of my early life and our family's*
> *history; I think this worthwhile, and I hope that these*
> *random notes may be interesting and revealing to you*
> *and of myself. As I try to search back in the deepest*
> *recesses of my memory—or, perhaps not so much of*

*memory as of recollections of what I was told of the
memories of others—I come up with the dialectic of
love and pleasure, and pain and grief, intertwined,
alternating and always and unpredictably mixed up
with each other.*

Maybe it was the scent of the vintage paper, but I felt as
though I were holding a relic, something far weightier than my
own, puny life. As I saw the names embedded in the neat lines
of type—my grandparents Muki and Csurka, my father's sister,
Aunt Csupi—I felt a twinge of guilt. They'd been pillars of my
childhood, but in the intervening years I'd barely thought of them
at all. In fact, some of them weren't even dead. Aunt Csupi was
still alive at the age of 92, nestled within the impeccably clean
bowels of a Swiss nursing home. But we hadn't spoken in years.

I read on. My father wrote with lawyerly precision, assem-
bling a neat portfolio of carefully curated memories. I'd forgotten
about the time when, half-drunk from eating fermented plums
at his Uncle Miklos' farm, he'd fallen off a ladder and knocked
himself out cold. Or how during a Sunday visit to Uncle Sandor's
machine shop, he let my father operate the giant lathe to turn a
little piece of scrap metal.

But scattered amidst these sepia-toned reflections were darker
ones. My father hinted at the fear that dogged his parents, and
the sense he was somehow different from the other, non-Jewish
kids. There were even moments drawn from his experience of
war: *A movie in slow motion but badly out of focus,* he wrote. But
we never get to the end: His recollections stop abruptly during
the Siege of Budapest, almost as if he'd been hit mid-sentence.

I put the papers down. There was something else about my
father's recollections, and the more I tried to shut it out the
more it troubled me: I no longer knew if I could trust him. For
all his descriptive skill, I couldn't ignore the inconsistencies in
his story. When I was a boy, he'd told me that after he emigrated

to the United States, he was so overcome by patriotic feeling that he'd volunteered for military service in Korea. Or the ear story: Supposedly, he'd lost some of his hearing during his military service, though the cause was never made quite clear. Was it due to an artillery shell misfiring in the turret of his tank, like he once told me when I was young? Or was it the result of a pressurization fault in a post-war transport flight, as he told me another time?

I'd never thought much about these little discrepancies, chalking them up instead to my father's absent-minded storytelling style. Now I couldn't let them go. I remembered a road trip back in 1995, when I was driving out to San Francisco to start a new life. Before my father's diagnosis.

The first evening, when I stopped at the Midwest home of a distant relative, I had an unanticipated reunion. As I stepped into the kitchen I ran smack into my father's first wife, Ruth. I wasn't prepared for this, and for a long moment I wasn't sure if I should just turn around and leave. I knew the marriage hadn't been a happy one, and that she still held my father in something lower than contempt. Instead, I offered a wan: "Uh, hi!"

"Hi," said Ruth, her eyes narrowing ever so slightly. "Welcome to Illinois."

We chit-chatted uneasily for a few minutes. Then—and I swear, I'll never know what prompted it—I let fly a breezy remark about his service in Korea. Maybe she could fill in some missing details.

Ruth's eyes flashed. "Korea?" she sneered. "*Bullshit!* He was never in Korea!"

Beneath my feet, the ground shifted ever so slightly.

"Are you...sure?" I choked out. Ruth's face had taken on the look of a large and dangerous bird. Behind her triumphant grin were decades of rage, and I certainly wasn't about to become an apologist for my father's...for his *what*, exactly? He couldn't have flat-out *lied*. Perhaps it was just a misunderstanding. Maybe she thought he said: "I'm going to *Peoria* to fight in the war, see you in a few months"?

But the moment passed. If I felt the need to seek clarification, it was a distant urge. I knew there'd be time to ask about it at some unnamed point in the future. Of course, I never did. Even in Florida, in those fleeting moments before he winked out forever, I could've pressed him. But it seemed cruel. He was already so weak, and the fact neither of us could acknowledge—that he was grateful to be leaving—lay between us like a lump of gristle.

Now, as I sat with my father's slim memoirs spread out before me, the decades pooled and swirled together around me. Which of his stories—if any of them—were true? Why had he obscured his backstory, and so clumsily at that? Behind this, another question: That as my own life felt shakier and less purposeful by the day, why was my only response to hide out in the basement with my hands over my eyes?

I didn't know. I didn't know whether my father was a liar, or if I'd ever feel like my life was on track. Had it ever been? When I looked back into the antechambers of my own memory, everything seemed murky and indistinct. The only times I'd really felt a sense of purpose was when I'd been in bands, and yet none of them had really panned out. My wife and daughter loved me, but it hardly mattered to me. Everything I'd been given, from whatever talent I possessed to the inheritance I was wasting, felt like they'd all been squandered.

I wondered how I felt about my predicament, and I realized that I didn't know. It was a long moment before I recognized it wasn't something I could look up in a book, or that anyone else could answer for me. I'd have to find out for myself.

6

Portland, March 2017: The therapist's name was Renee. A woman roughly my age, sharp-featured and trim, long hair pulled into an orderly bun. She greeted us warmly and gestured us into her office. Julianna and I sat down warily on the couch. "So," Renee said, her voice as precise as her hair, "Tell me a little about why you're here."

It was Julianna who'd blinked first. A few weeks before, she'd sat me down on the edge of our bed. "I can't take this anymore," she said. "This isn't working. We need to try something new or we need to give up."

She'd never felt this distant before. After her naturopath identified the source of her mysterious illness—a gut disorder called "SIBO" that prevented her from absorbing the nutrients in her food—Julianna had started seeing the shaman, who used Brazilian chants and capoeira moves to try and uncover the spiritual roots of the illness. I hardly cared that he was using his cockeyed magic to lead her into deeper and deeper realms of herself, or that she and I hadn't had sex in months. It wasn't so much we'd fallen out of love; I wasn't sure we'd ever been in it. Surely this was proof we were simply two good people stuck in the wrong marriage.

"I dunno," I said, desperate to avoid this confrontation. "Do you really need someone else to tell you I'm the wrong person for you?" This was a tactic I'd settled on in the last few months: Pointing out all the ways *I* was wrong for *her*. Judging from the rage it tended to inspire, it wasn't working.

"Why are you doing this?" she said, her eyes narrowing in anger. "What do you really want?"

"I don't understand what you're talking about," I answered, my blood rising. The question enraged me, because I had no satisfactory answer. "I want to succeed, to feel like I matter. Instead, I feel like…I barely exist."

"Seth," said Julianna. "Look at me." There was no mistaking the tenderness in her voice, but undergirding it was a hard rime of despair. "I'm going to make an appointment with Renee," she went on. "We have to find a different way, or we need to step away from each other gracefully and figure out how to raise our kid."

Ending up alone in middle age would be the perfect fulfillment of my widower fantasy: Tragic and pitiable, yet praiseworthy in its stoic denial of need. Some part of me knew it was wrong. But disastrous though splitting up would be for the three of us, most of all for our daughter, I couldn't envision another ending. In the brief moments I could be honest with myself I recognized that, really, this was what I wanted: For Julianna to exit the scene, even for her to die. *How had it come to this?* My circuits flooded by a paralyzing wave of inputs, I had no idea what I should do. Now that we were finally in Renee's office, the answer felt even more distant.

Julianna answered her first. "We love each other, that's not in doubt," she said, throwing a glance my way. "We've had a long history together, much of it wonderful. But we can't go on like this. It feels more like we're roommates than a married couple. There's so much of him I don't know. Music used to be our language, but I have a spiritual hunger I can't deny, and Seth won't meet me there.

"There's all this tenderness here, but there are also these massive holes where I feel like I don't know anything about him. I think it has something to do with the people who raised him and his mother dying, but we can't even touch that. From the healing work I'm doing, I know the past isn't the past. Sometimes it feels like our house is crawling with ghosts. It's heavy, and there's no joy, and I'm exhausted trying to chase this person who doesn't want to be found."

Renee turned to me. After a moment, I spoke. "It's true, I love Julianna with all my heart. I don't think I've ever met anyone kinder. But more and more, I feel like she wants someone different. Someone like her who reads the *Bhagavad Gita,* who meditates at dawn and does yoga. I just feel like I'm the wrong person for her."

"I get it," said Renee. "So…what do you want from your marriage?"

Blood thrummed in my temples. We were finally here, on the couch, and still I had no answer.

"I…I'm a private person. I just want to…I don't know, to feel like I'm doing something with my life. That I'm succeeding, that I'm making progress."

"Progress towards what?" asked Renee.

"Towards mattering. Towards doing something…constructive." No one had to point out how lame this sounded.

The room was quiet and still, afternoon sunlight peeking through slatted blinds. Help was so close at hand, and yet I couldn't unclench my arms from around my chest. A vision spun inside me: Me sitting in my basement studio, surrounded by the dim light of antique vacuum tubes. Alone in my underground bunker, where maybe I'd finally start making the music I never seemed to begin.

"Could I have a glass of water?" I asked.

The rest of that session, and the next one, ground on like this. Soon the talk turned to how to go about the process of separating, to make it as kind and respectful as we could. That's when Renee surprised us both.

"How would you feel," she said at the end of our second meeting, "about trying a session under the influence of MDMA?"

For a moment I was too surprised to say anything. I looked instead at her bookshelf, where a copy of *Psychedelic Psychiatry* perched innocently alongside the DSM.

"Uh...wow," I said. "I mean, sure...I guess?" Why was I so hesitant? I knew that LSD, before it'd been classified a drug of abuse by the DEA, had been used in countless therapy sessions well into the '60s. And while I insisted my own teenaged "experiments" were purely for recreational purposes, they often yielded insights that persisted into the bleary days afterwards.

Julianna didn't hesitate. "Totally," she said, turning to me. "Did you ever read that *New Yorker* piece on Johns Hopkins? What do we have to lose?"

"Um, okay."

Just like that, it was settled. That night, I woke up in the pre-dawn light and got up to use the bathroom. As I paused before the mirror, I studied my reflection. My own face looked unfamiliar, its contours merging with those who'd come before me. *Who was I?* I heard the faintest of whispers—*was that my grandmother Csurka murmuring in soft Hungarian?*—hectoring and scolding me from some far-off place. A tape loop someone had forgotten to switch off.

Two weeks later, Julianna and I drove through gloomy late-Saturday rain to Renee's office. My heart pounded heavily in the quiet darkness. If you'd seen me that evening and asked where I was going, I'd have told you it was to the firing squad.

7

Portland, April 2017: When Julianna and I entered Renee's office, the room we'd known only in daylight had been transformed. Now the walls were lit by soft electric candlelight. Nests of blankets and pillows beckoned us to the floor, not the couch. I sat down and made myself comfortable, so much as my thumping heart would allow.

Renee had transformed as well. In daylight, she exuded a blend of warmth and incisiveness, never leaving a thought unfinished. Now the precision of her clinical persona had softened to a witchy energy. No longer sure just who she was or what her role was, I toggled between excitement and unease. But Julianna's eager calm radiated out to me. If nothing else, we were somewhere—anywhere—besides our dark house, circling each other like prisoners.

Renee sat down with us and produced two tiny baggies. Inside each were two capsules, one to take now and one in a couple of hours. I looked at them. They didn't seem particularly magical. Julianna and I looked at each other. I said: "This is really it," or something equally dumb, not even knowing what I meant. The end? The beginning? I'd never doubted that I loved her; she just wanted someone different, someone more like her. Someone who loved nature, who was bolder and more expressive than I was. That was okay, I reasoned; some people just weren't meant to be together, and now we were facing the fact that we were those people.

"Deepest knowing, deepest healing, deepest medicine," said Renee. Julianna and I looked at each other squarely. We raised our water glasses to each other, and then we each swallowed the first pills.

For what felt like far too long, nothing happened. Julianna, Renee, and I sat in our pillowy nests. The electric candles threw their soft shadows over the walls. Inside, I quelled my fear by imagining the life I would soon be living: Alone in the house my wife and daughter had once occupied, surrounded by the recording gear I'd so painstakingly collected. Alone, with all the time and space I needed to write the music I never actually seemed to finish, to fix the piles of broken amplifiers I never actually seemed to use. It would be perfect. The complications of this vision—*What will this do to Evelyn? How will we afford to keep the house when we barely earn enough to scrape by?*—felt reassuringly distant.

The clock dripped on. Now a subtle shift unfolded, a quickening and a softening. Some gentle hand passed over the top of my head, and as it did my thoughts of the future receded behind a heavy curtain. There is only the present. I sit in silence for a while until a distant part of my body beckons: my bladder, which boasts the capacity of a single-shot espresso cup. I rise and pad down the hall to the bathroom. Now I recognize a new tilt to the floor, a gentle flex in my joints as I stop by the mirror and study my reflection a few beats too long. I know that MDMA isn't a hallucinogen; I don't see contrails splitting the air or an electric grid overlaid across my vision. But a curious thrumming comes over me, even as my musculature and bones begin to sag and liquify just a little. I hurry back to the office.

Warmth. Sitting back into the blanket of my nest, I'm held in soft light. Julianna lies shaking on the floor underneath her blanket, the therapist kneeling next to her. I have never seen this happen before, her entire body twitching and jerking, eyes closed and that beautiful face upturned. I find myself afraid, worried that something's gone wrong, that something is being let in or let out that shouldn't be. Renee turns and sends a comforting look my way. Everything is okay. Everything is good.

The final glimmers of daylight throw a spectral glow over the room. I'm fully caught in the medicine's undertow now, my joints cushioned as if by thick oil. Dry lips, slow movements, a gentle drift into some new and warm place, fear dropping away like molted and spent feathers. I have the distinct sense I'm less leaving my body than entering it for the first time. I've never brought my consciousness here, not in quite this way: to the inside of myself. I'm gently being shaken awake, and I feel a new architecture inside me, bodies within my body. Clear glass tubes and pipettes, spotless porcelain arteries through which I tumble, ever deeper inside.

Earlier, in my ordinary state, my mind spun stories of my essential brokenness. Now, inside me is the beautiful machine of me, and I feel a welcome wholeness. Not broken, not cursed. Not different in my essentials from anyone else. Everything I say I'm waiting for—that moment on the vanishing horizon when things magically come together—it waits patiently for me. All the stories of time wasted and opportunities missed are only stories, ones I have told myself in order to maintain my illusion of tragedy.

Now a new story rises up. This one is about my mother, and I know that it's true. It's that Friday evening, the night she left for the hospital and never came back. I am four and a half years old. Sitting at the top of the staircase, I feel the nubby crunch of carpeting beneath my flannel pajamas. Below me, on the landing by the front door, my father is bundling my mother in a shawl. She turns towards me and I see that her face is ashen and drawn, her eyes wide. My mother is scared, scared out of her wits. I see that now. There is no false cheer here, no "Don't worry, I'll be back soon!" I do not recall any words passing between us at all. The frame stops now, the details frozen. Dried eucalyptus in an earthenware jar; the wood-framed mirror on the wall. My parents turn back to the door. The scene repeats, locked now in endless loop. Me, the door. The door, me. I recognize with merciful softness that this is the last time I can be certain I saw her. It is tender, this memory. It is deeply sad. But it is also a gift, a tiny glimpse into an earlier me, not the broken one. It is painless. Not numb. Painless.

Far away, in the therapist's office, the storm passing through Julianna's body has lifted. I bob back up to the surface too, held in the warm embrace of the candlelit room. To my side, my wife stirs in her blanketed nest, then sleepily pulls herself upright. Although she's already a physically beautiful woman, something extra shines through her now, a radiance illumining her fine-boned face, those wondrous, bottomless blue eyes. She looks into my own and says with quiet and total clarity: "I don't want to get a divorce."

8

Portland, April 2017: With a soft *thump*, the movie playing behind my eyes skips off the sprocket: *There's my wife and daughter driving away from our house; there's me sitting in the basement surrounded by piles of broken guitars.* Future movie-memories. But I do not choose them.

I look into Julianna's eyes. They have an unearthly and wide-pupiled radiance now; I know that's the medicine at work. But something else is at play, a subtle melding. I am not seeing through her eyes, yet somehow we've become a *We*. There is no effort required; it simply is. It is shocking in its simplicity.

I am standing with her in the kitchen of our San Francisco apartment, twenty years before. I'm asking her to join with me, to be my partner. Some half-lit part of me knows that if she says *yes*, if she agrees to this, we won't have an easy time of it. Our wounds and our demons will rise up to challenge us and hold us apart. We will run deep into primeval forests to escape one another, climb icy mountain passes, anything to avoid that final surrender. But it will not be for nothing, this crucible. If we manage to stay together, if stubborn will or inertia or even something like faith holds us together, something tells me that beyond this there awaits a wide-openness, a self-knowing and a love greater than any I could possibly imagine.

Now, held in the medicine's embrace, my body thrums with a simple knowing: That we are not here to suffer each other.

That our souls have some contract to fulfill, that we're here for a deeper purpose. We hang there together, up in the clouds. All the tragic stories I've told about us are dropping away, beautiful withered leaves that have served their purpose, ready now for mulching.

We ride the waves of the medicine together. Quiet music, soft blankets, cooling draughts of coconut water and almond milk to counteract the medicine's thermostatic charge. Sometimes Renee offers gentle guidance. "Can you feel the wisdom of your protectors?" she asks me. "The parts of you that kept you hidden and safe?" I can. Then she goes quiet for long stretches and I worry, perversely, if she's bored.

Mostly I sit in quiet awe. I feel my heart coming online with dawning and unexpected capability, and I'm genuinely surprised. *My heart?* This isn't an organ I've allowed myself to orient towards, and for a moment I long for my cynical facade. But I can't deny the medicine's deep magic. It's illuminating what some deeper aspect of me—a part I've never dared to name: *my soul*—knows to be true. I feel a deep, full-body trust in myself that is as foreign as it is exhilarating. There is no second-guessing it.

This night will end, as all nights must. The medicine runs its course, and eight hours after we arrived, Julianna and I hug and thank Renee effusively and walk out into Portland's deserted downtown. Julianna and I return to our empty home—Evelyn is with her grandmother tonight—and quietly remove our clothing, brush our teeth, and climb into bed, just like we always do. But we are not the same people who left it.

We are not "cured." In the months to follow Julianna and I will continue to fight, to blame each other for our shortcomings, even to contemplate splitting up once or twice more. But neither of us can unsee what we've seen, unfeel what we've felt. For all my native creativity, I've never stopped to consider how much of my identity—the things I thought were innately "me"—might be stories: Stories I've told about myself, been told about myself, overheard my parents and grandparents telling about me. Is it too late to change them? As sleep overtakes me, the sense of possibility is a quiet but insistent current running through my body. I know this much: This wondrous state has awakened something, returned Julianna and I to our essential contract with one another. From this night forward, nothing will be the same again.

9

Portland, April 2017: A friend once shared a terrifying description of depression with me. "It's not like the lights go out," he told me. "It's like entering a dark room and turning them *on*."

Now I knew what he meant. In those first days after the "medicine"—no one who dispenses therapeutic MDMA calls it a "drug"—I felt the walls around me dissolving. It wasn't like those high school flashbacks, when equations on the blackboard would suddenly rearrange themselves, or time itself seem to skip a frame. But when Julianna and I returned from Renee's office that night, everything seemed different, as if I'd somehow been bleached.

Renee had warned us about this, how the serotonin crash can leave you feeling aimless and hollow. I wasn't depressed, but now I couldn't unsee all the glaring discordances I'd woven through my life. No wonder my beautiful recording studio sat unused: Whether due to my middling musical aptitude or my essential inwardness, my lack of success wasn't a fluke. My conception of myself—*an engineer! a composer!*—was merely a story, and not a very believable one.

It is exquisitely painful to wake up halfway through your life to feel as though you've done it all wrong. Still, I wasn't hopeless. One of MDMA's gifts is that it fosters something called "fear memory extinction," a state in which it's easier to revisit painful or even traumatic memories in an objective way. And it doesn't end when the medicine wears off. In the conversations that followed that first MDMA session, Renee explained that the work occurs less in the medicine state than in the days, weeks, and even months that follow. "The medicine is very effective in revealing those buried backstories, those hidden traumas and splits," she said. "But it can't do the work of actually integrating them. That's *our* job."

These revelations sometimes came in surprising forms. During an evening bath a few days after that first session, Julianna had a vision. "I just had this…I don't know, a visitation?" she said as she toweled off. "It was like a dream. I'd just laid back and closed my eyes when the women in your family—your mother Rhonda, your stepmother Irene, Grandma Csurka and Aunt Csupi—they all came to me in a procession. Each of them had a basket, but they weren't carrying offerings. Instead it was like a picnic of the sacrifices each of them had to endure.

"Your family," she added, not unkindly, "is not an easy one to marry into."

"That's an understatement," I said. Inside me, gears were turning. If she'd come to me with this a week before, I probably would've rolled my eyes. Julianna had never met any of those women; she knew them only from photographs and my own scanty reminiscences. But now I felt curious. For one thing, she was right: The women in my family *had* all gotten pretty raw deals. And Julianna *was* one of them, just as I was connected to the family members who'd come before me. Something began to click over inside, the notion that I was no longer just an unconscious actor.

This is when life began to get trippy.

Even now, I'm not sure how to describe it. Nothing changed on the outside. I still lived in the same house, ate the same kinds of food, took our daughter to the bus stop each morning and picked her up in the afternoon. But everything was different. It was like the walls had been revealed to be made of sand. Sometimes I'd reach out and touch them, hoping the rough plaster might somehow reassure me. But some part of me was reaching right through them, into some place beyond my comprehension. I couldn't see it, but I knew it was there. Was it the walls that were changing, or me?

Julianna's vision reignited a dim memory of my own. Twenty years before, when Deborah, Stacey, and I cleared out the family home in Washington, I'd chanced upon a letter my mother had written to my father. I remembered being struck by it, the only example I'd ever seen of my mother's handwriting. But then I tucked it away and forgot about it. Now I went out to the garage and began to root around in a dusty plastic bin. Finally I found a battered paper folder with a typewritten label: "Rhonda G. Lorinczi." I brought it inside and spread the contents out on the living room floor.

True to form, my father had saved every slip of paper relating to my mother's death: Insurance forms, social security benefits for Stacey and me, shocked letters of condolence in English, French, Italian, and Hungarian. Here was a crinkled *Washington Post* article noting the unusualness of my mother's case, how hardly anyone died of encephalitis in the United States, least of all a seemingly healthy 37-year-old. A photo from my parents' wedding: My mother stands stiff-backed in an ugly plastic neck brace. Now I remembered there'd been a traffic accident of some kind. I was struck by the resonance with my own wedding: Just like Julianna, my mother had come to the altar a cripple.

Finally, underneath an autopsy report from the Armed Forces Institute of Pathology, I found the letter. The stationery was from "The Westbury," a hotel in downtown Chicago. Nice stuff, too: Rising Line Marque rag paper. The letters were cursive and stylized, written in green felt-tip pen. But these artful touches did nothing to soften the content:

> *"Living with you is trying, you must be dimly aware... evasive, opaque, obtuse. I am ready to explode most of the time. I feel an enemy within my garden. Sly, misleading, but also sweet and loving and good. Bafflement. Confusion. Why? I cannot feel you, see you with unjaded, sympathetic eyes when in the midst of struggle with you. Yet I do want our marriage—So how to do it?" —RGL*

Underneath the date—March 12, 1974—my mother had written "Wesley Mem. Hosp." Was it related to her neck brace? Was one of her parents having a medical procedure? I didn't know. All I had were these meaningless details: Where the hotel was, the quality of the hotel stationery. And the fury leaching off the page like dioxin. Did she believe her letter would shock him out of his protective shell, or was she already planning for a life after him? She never got to find out. A year and a half later, she was dead.

The last time I'd really asked about my mother was back in Florida, when my father was dying. One night Deborah and I sat in the living room listening to the murmur of the sea. With my father asleep, it seemed easier to ask the questions that somehow never seemed right to ask in daylight. Ones about my mother, and who she'd really been.

"You know, I was really dazzled by Rhonda," Deborah told me. "She was so stylish and brilliant. *Wicked* brilliant. But your dad and I didn't really get her, either. She was just, like, so far out ahead."

"You mean, like her car?"

"Yes! You remember the yellow Porsche; she was such hot shit! Like, this one night we were all out at dinner. Rhonda was talking about her dating history, in college. And she said—really breezy, like it was no big deal—that before your dad, most if not all of her partners had been female. And you know what? Your dad and I didn't say a word. We just put our heads down and ate our dinners. We literally didn't say a word."

I didn't say anything, either. My mother suddenly seemed both far more and far less real than she had. Why had no one told me anything about her? Why hadn't I bothered to ask?

"In fact," Deborah went on, "I totally forgot about it. But a few months later, Rhonda took me to a doctor's appointment or something, and in the elevator she turned to me and asked 'Did what I said at dinner that night upset you?' I literally had no idea what she was talking about. I couldn't remember it even happening."

I was silent. The only sound was the distant roar of the ocean outside. I recognized that I could literally count my definitive memories of my mother on one hand. Now everything I thought I'd known was being blown into shards of mirrored glass.

Like so much about my time in Florida, in the twenty years since then I'd more or less forgotten it. Now I felt a slow drip of sadness working through me. Before she'd met my father, my mother had been one of only a handful of female attorneys working in the field of gender equity. But then she abandoned her law practice to bear him two children. What else did she give up?

Striver. Contrarian. Devoted wife. Lapsed lesbian. I knew next to nothing about my mother and now this knowing, or its absence, hit me. A question cautiously formed itself, gently at first, then pressing with greater insistence. Having already surrendered so much, what if my mother had simply done the reasonable thing? What if she'd just let go of the rope?

In the weeks that followed that first MDMA session I pondered this question, and others I'd never dared ask. This fractal time was hard. I saw how far I'd strayed from my essential self, and it seemed the only way forward was down. And so I dove ever deeper into my father's memoirs, into those half-lit chambers of memory. Maybe they'd tell me how I'd ended up here, and where I should turn next.

PART TWO

Into the Dark

Muki at the Alpine Front, 1915 - 16

10

Portland, June 2017: The whole of that long, strange summer, I felt like a deep-sea diver dropping into an abyssal and uncharted trench. As my father's memoirs guided me ever deeper, tiny glimmers of memory flashed like silver fins before disappearing into the lightless depths. As I read the long-forgotten names of long-dead relatives—Miklos, Desző, and others still—my own childhood felt far closer than it had, the world somehow smaller. A few weeks before, I could barely remember my grandparents. Now a new world was revealing itself to me, and it seemed vital that I understand where I'd come from.

I began with my grandfather. His given name was Eugene, but everyone called him Muki (for "chap" or "fellow"). I remember him, barely: a prominent forehead, antique horn-rims perched on an unsubtle nose. His face, slender and gently rounded in a way I associate with Hungarianness, framed shy but kind eyes. He died in July of 1975, when I was four. But as I bolstered my father's slim recollections with history books and copious web searches, a snapshot of Muki's early life came into view. And it was clear it hadn't been a happy one.

Let me tell you what I know about the childhood and formative years of my father, Muki. For an open and honest parent, my dad was strangely reluctant to speak to me about his early childhood. I suspect that this was due not only to the painful nature of his recollections, but also to a degree of shame about circumstances he considered unbecoming of our family.

My grandfather was born in 1894 in Kisvárda, a whistle stop on the *puzsta*, the grasslands that frame the western edge of the Eurasian steppe. A quiet and bookish boy, Muki couldn't have chosen a worse location. The *puzsta* is Hungary's version of Big Sky country; its inhabitants were once Europe's cowboys, earning a meager living herding their *Magyar Szürke*, the photogenic longhorns that have grazed these lands for over 1,000 years. During off hours the men drank, gambled, and fought in taverns lit by greasy lanterns, daggers tucked in the cuffs of their boots. Just as in our own iconic frontier, the culture of the *puszta* was coarse and intolerant. Violence, often sexual, was woven into the very fabric of life.

Jews lived here once, too. Onion sellers, rag men, knife sharpeners and the like, dressed in shirts of white linen, waistcoats and tunics of rough black cloth. Muki's father, my great-grandfather Ignacz, was a *kupec*—an itinerant trader—renting out farming equipment during the harvest season. A large, handsome man with an impressive mustache, Ignacz considered his four children no impediment to his pursuit of philandery, or the faint odor of disreputability which clung to him like dung.

You know that Ignacz Lorinczi—my grandfather—was something of a roué, at least by the standards of that age, perhaps by any standards. All Muki would tell me was that his large family lived in poverty, frequently moving and finally splitting up by having him going to

*live with relatives in Nagyvárad, a largely Hungarian
city in Transylvania, now called Oradea in Romania.*

There was something else. As I searched for information on Kisvárda and the nearby towns, a pattern began to emerge. Most places had an awkwardly translated web page highlighting a point of minor interest: a museum or an historic church. But eventually I'd come to the same words repeated more or less verbatim: "Before World War II, Kisvárda (or *Eger, or Győr, or Kőszeg*) had a large Jewish community. They were confined to a ghetto in 1944, and then deported to Auschwitz. The majority perished there. Today there are almost no Jews in Kisvárda (*or Abony, or Heves, or Mohács*)." I'd soon learn that, though Hungary was the last place to be subjected to the Holocaust, the devastation it wrought there was astonishingly total. Outside Budapest, roughly nine out of ten Jews perished. And yet all four of my father's immediate family survived. How?

Muki was born in a fortuitous moment. In 1867, roughly thirty years before his birth, the Jews of Hungary were offered an historic opportunity. That year, Hungary entered into a union with Austria called the Dual Monarchy, initiating a reshuffling of ethnic and political blocs. The Magyars, who considered themselves the "true" Hungarians, needed to demonstrate they represented a majority share of the population. And for this they needed the Jews.

For centuries, Jews had been a barely tolerated underclass. Now they were granted full legal emancipation and they responded with patriotic fervor, flocking to the merchant, cultural, and political classes. Later, historians would call this the "Golden Era," an epoch of harmony and tolerance. It also afforded a brainy young Jew like my grandfather a path forward: An education. And so Muki was sent to Nagyvárad to study.

Nagyvárad was a center of culture and education, it must have seemed like heaven after the dust and cow shit of Kisvárda. The chief of police was Jewish, as were many merchants, manufacturers, lawyers and physicians. But if Muki's horizons were expanding, his time here wasn't exactly carefree. My father devoted only a handful of sentences to his father's adolescence, but it was impossible to miss the through line:

> *This was, clearly, a very painful period in my dad's life. He lived, I suspect, the life of a poor, supernumerary relation with an obviously middle-class family of whom I know nothing. He compensated for this, I believe, by studying with great energy and formidable dedication, and finishing near the top of his class.*

I'd never considered that my grandfather had once been young, or harbored any concerns beyond the tidiness of his reading nook or his daily allotment of three cigarettes, Kent brand. He was just a shrunken figure in old-man clothes. Now I realized how punishing his early life had been, how hard he'd had to work to claw himself up from penury. He'd surmounted so much: his impoverished childhood and wastrel of a father, the shame of being dependent upon distant relatives. Earning his diploma—an achievement fewer than one in twenty Hungarians could then claim—had changed all that. It was June of 1914, and for a brief and breathless moment, Muki stood at the very edge of the world.

At that moment, some 350 miles to the south, Sarajevo readied itself for a visit from Archduke Franz Ferdinand, the presumptive heir to the Austro-Hungarian throne.

11

> *I cannot tell you much more about Csurka's early years; she was fourteen when her father died a sudden and heroic death. He was the stationmaster of a small railway*

center in northern Hungary when, on a late evening in December 1914, some instinct told him to return to the control tower, where he noticed that an eastbound troop train and a westbound hospital train returning from the Russian front were somehow switched onto the same track, heading for a collision. He grabbed a red lantern and ran a mile in bitter cold and snow to succeed in halting the trains just in time before dropping dead of a heart attack. I hope he received his reward in heaven, because his family sure as hell did not receive it on this earth: a posthumous decoration and a very small pension for my grandmother Helen and her two children.

Portland, July 2017: My grandmother Csurka died when I was eleven; she even lived with us for a year or two, after Muki died. But my recollections of my grandmother weren't exactly warm. Csurka was the master of the sharp word and the slap on the wrist, either of which she could wield with shocking speed and authority. She categorized my numerous deficiencies as *schlumpus,* a word whose meaning was neither offered nor required. Csurka's sourness seemed to spring not from the passion of anger but a broader, almost elemental denial of happiness. I recognized even as a child it would never be penetrated, though I never understood why. My father revered her, and he'd spend his life courting, marrying, divorcing, or burying fierce, hard-assed women in a fruitless bid at reunion.

Csurka's given name was "Janka"—Jane—but like most Hungarians, she took a nickname: Csurka, or "ponytail." I didn't know much about her childhood, but I know that after her father's sudden death, her family's finances became precarious, her mother Helen scrambling to make ends meet.

There was one other thing: Before she'd met Muki, Csurka had loved someone else, a local boy. During the First World War, he was called up and posted to the Eastern Front, only a few hundred miles away. There, the Army's blunderous leadership would bestow on the Austro-Hungarians the highest casualty rate of any combatant in the war. Over the course of three disastrous weeks in 1914, some 100,000 of them would die in pointless charges against massed machine guns, hurled like fistfuls of sand against the Russians, again and again, until there were no men left to throw. My grandmother's first love was one of them. I don't know where or when he died; I don't even know his name. But I saw now that, just as in Muki's case, uncertainty and loss had defined most of my grandmother's life.

As I began to metabolize my grandparents' stories, they pinged something deep inside me. For as long as I could remember, there'd been a voice in my head. Not a literal one exactly, but an imaginary figure I just thought of as "the Voice." (Not the most inspired name, but whatever.) I'd never really questioned it because, well, if it were in my head, it must be…me, right? And it was there to help me. Never mind that all it seemed to do was to criticize, always reminding me of the things I'd failed to follow through on, the chances I should've taken but hadn't. *This is your only chance,* it told me, and over the years I'd taken it to heart, insisting on an anxious perfectionism that never really seemed to get me anywhere.

Something came into focus now. I wondered if the Voice had come from somewhere outside me; if it did, I had a hunch my grandparents had something to do with it. Whatever they'd lived through, whatever had molded and shaped them, it might live on in me as well. I'd been living this way for forty years, never the wiser. Was it too late to change?

12

Portland, July 2017: "Jesus, it's like you're moving in slow motion!" Julianna growled. "The goddamn ferry isn't going to wait for us."

It was the morning of our annual camping trip to Orcas Island. Every summer a group of seventy-odd Portlanders trek up to the San Juans and spend a week in a state camp. The only challenge is getting there: Depending on traffic, driving through Seattle can be a nightmare or a breeze. And the ferry reservation, booked months in advance, wasn't transferrable. Everything hinged on getting out the door on time. And right now, that didn't seem likely.

As Julianna bustled in fast motion all around me—emptying the fridge, stuffing sleeping bags into the back of our car—I hucked a few pieces of gear into the car and crept downstairs to my basement studio. Here, held in this quiet cocoon, Julianna's simmering rage faded to a distant roar. *No wonder we never go on trips,* I thought. My skin felt prickly and soft, like it might suddenly break open.

Once we were on the road, I endured the first ten minutes of the drive in icy silence. It wasn't until we'd merged onto I-5 that Julianna finally composed herself enough to address me. "What the hell was going on back there?" she asked. "It's like you're deliberately trying to thwart me." Behind us Evelyn, all of ten years old, stared fixedly out the window, headphones jammed over her ears.

"I really wasn't. It's just incredibly stressful to be around you when you're like that. I feel like I can only do it wrong."

"So tell me," said Julianna, her words sparking with anger, "why do you move so slow?"

"When things get stressful, it helps me get my feet under me. So I don't spin out."

Inside, I grasped at more excuses why it was necessary for me to retreat inside my shell. So I was unprepared for what Julianna said next: "Does that remind you of anything from your childhood?"

I paused a beat to be sure I'd understood her. *Was this a trap?* Then I said: "My stepmother. She was so anxious and brittle. The way she'd openly mock my father when things weren't going her way. So she'd have some way of getting back at him."

After a moment I asked: "What about you?"

"It reminds me of when I was a kid. My mom would go on these crazy tears, cleaning and rearranging stuff. I'd try to do her chores for her, to make it easier for her, but it just seemed to make her angrier. She could be so merciless to my dad sometimes. Like she just hated him."

"It's no wonder we do this shit. And no wonder I want to disappear. It seems so obvious now, but…. I really wasn't trying to mess with you. I just…I don't know how to collaborate with you when everything's that tense. It's just so much easier to disappear."

"Like your father?"

"Like my father."

We drove the next few miles in silence. I felt the same sense I had in those first days after MDMA, when so many of the things I counted on felt no more solid than water. My father's image rose inside me now, the rounded features and soft eyes I thought I'd known so well. *Who had he really been? Who, for that matter, was I?* As we picked our way through the gauntlet of Seattle traffic, that question faded to a reassuringly distant hum. The conversation turned to the week to come: Who we'd run into on the ferry, how long it would be before the kids were consumed with pranking each other. My mood lightened, and I recognized how much I'd needed this unscripted break from regular life.

We pulled in to the Anacortes ferry terminal with forty-five minutes to spare. As the vessel lurched into ponderous motion I made my way up to the bow. Alone for a moment, I savored the buffeting of the wind. All around me was an awe-inspiring view: The islands of Puget Sound forming a semicircle around us, the Canadian shoreline only a few miles to the north. The sky was cobalt, the air brisk. It was a vista my water-loving father would have delighted in, and now a memory swam back to me.

When I was a boy, my father owned a powerboat on the Potomac River. Sometimes we'd cruise to the river's terminus where it opens into the vastness of the Chesapeake Bay. My father was captivated by this place, where the water's not quite salt and not quite fresh. It's called *brackish*. It's more metaphor than place; some creatures become disoriented within it, while others tolerate its gauzy boundaries with ease. Here, freed from the strictures of life on shore, my father would relax a little, almost becoming someone else. "Look over there," he told me once, pointing to a disembodied mast on the horizon. "The Bay is so wide you can see the curvature of the earth as ships approach from the other side." His voice was tinged with a childlike wonder, and in such moments I knew he was here—all the way here. They were among the happiest of my entire childhood.

Now, standing at the ferry's windswept bow, I felt the bittersweetness of these memories. How when things got hard, my father would simply leave, retreating to his bedroom or extended work trips abroad. But even when he was gone, his absence was a presence, a father-shaped void one could never forget. It was, I saw now, a passive form of control, a way to ensure he remained the center of attention without actually having to be present.

The fight with Julianna that morning had shaken me, and yet something was different. For all the ways it felt like we were reading from some ancient script, neither of us had collapsed into anguish or resentment. Those nights in MDMA—we'd sat three sessions by now—had broken something loose. I didn't know the way forward, but at least I knew there *was* one. I glanced back to the cabin, where Julianna and Evelyn sat in the glorious late-afternoon sunshine, and I felt my heart swelling in gratitude.

13

Orcas Island, July 2017: As the Orcas Island ferry terminal drew close, we descended belowdecks and got back in our car. There's no cell reception in the middle of Puget Sound, and now Julianna's phone dinged with a voicemail alert. After listening to it, she turned to me with a bemused expression: "That was the woman Renee connected me with. I've been invited to sit in that ayahuasca ceremony next month!"

I glanced reflexively at our daughter sitting behind us, but she had her headphones on. I knew that if she heard us there'd be no getting out of an awkward explanation, and I was pretty sure I wasn't ready to explain psychedelics to a ten-year-old. Maybe not even to myself. If what Renee had said was true, in Portland ayahuasca circles were about as common as artisanal donut shops. It seemed inevitable I'd encounter someone who drank it sooner or later; I just never thought it'd be my wife.

I admired her pluck. As a teenaged psychonaut I'd been warned above all to avoid "the bad trip." As far as I could tell, ayahausca *was* the bad trip: A pitiless and unblinking survey of one's life choices. Still, part of me was intrigued. According to Renee, ayahuasca was first brewed by Amazonian shamans thousands of years ago. How they knew that combining two unrelated plants—the *banisteriopsis caapi* vine and the *chacruna* shrub—would transform the inactive DMT in the shrub into a potent and long-lasting hallucinogen remains a poetic, and likely unsolvable mystery.

Then there were the physical effects. Ayahuasca often makes its drinkers vomit, sometimes violently. They might even lose control of their bowels. This was a hard red line (or, I suppose, a brown one) I was unwilling to cross. As if the opportunity to know oneself more deeply wasn't worth the discomfort of throwing up into a bucket, I convinced myself that ayahuasca simply wasn't for me.

We drove on towards camp, cresting rolling hills and dipping into luscious valleys dotted with bemused-looking cows. "So, the woman said there's only room for one right now, but that another place might open up," said Julianna, fixing me with a devilish look. "Want to come along? We could throw up together; it'd be so romantic!"

"Um…I don't know. Frankly, it sounds kind of terrifying. I mean, I guess if there were a spot for me.…"

I let the thought trail off as the turnoff for the campground appeared up ahead. There'd be time to dodge that bullet some other day, I reasoned, and with that I put the thought of ayahuasca out of my head. I thought instead about the week to come: walking the wooded trails, swimming and sailing, and eating well. Soon we were consumed by reunions, greeting old friends with hugs and smiles. After helping unload the car to the minimum extent possible, Evelyn ran off to join her friends at the lake. I felt better already; maybe this was the only medicine I needed.

The next morning, Julianna and I woke up early and walked down to the lake. With no one else around, we peeled off our clothes and jumped in. The sun had barely risen and the surface of the water was glasslike and serene. A short distance away, a trio of otters capered and dove amongst the kelp beds. Far across the lake a bald eagle cruised the shoreline searching for breakfast. We climbed out, got dressed, and walked around the edge of the water until we came to the boulder Julianna liked to meditate on. We hunkered down and listened as birdcalls and quiet splashes echoed all around us.

"You know, I have to be honest," she said. "It's so sweet to be here and goof off, but I'm struggling with small talk right now. I feel a little like an alien. Like I've crossed over."

I bristled a bit at this, though I wasn't sure why. "Okay, maybe it's not a perfect fit, but…I feel at home here. Like I belong to something. Like I'm at least half-normal."

"Maybe that's enough, then. Maybe it's enough to practice utopian living here. But I just think there's something deeper, someplace else."

Julianna was right, of course. Though we'd caught the merest glimpses of what lay ahead, the road hadn't yet risen up to meet us. Renee had warned us that once our lives began to change, some friends and relationships might no longer make sense to us. Afraid to lose the fragile feeling of belonging I felt, I was unwilling to let go of my former life.

If I couldn't name what was happening, I certainly felt it. When people asked me what I'd been up to, I found myself hedging. "Um, you know…fixing up the studio. Trying to find more scoring work." It felt too vulnerable to admit that Julianna and I had spent the last years in struggle, or that we'd been taking MDMA in therapy. Some part of me knew that it wouldn't play well here, that revealing something so tender and new might stifle it before it'd taken hold. And so I focused on my surroundings instead: The soft water of a mountain lake, the thick blanket of stars that bloomed above our heads each night. I thrilled at the sight of my daughter enfolded in a gaggle of good-hearted kids, and at the way Julianna's natural calm somehow set others at ease. Here, away from the heaviness I felt in Portland, I felt closer to her than I had in a long, long time.

The days dribbled languidly until suddenly it was all over. The last night I felt a familiar Sunday-night sadness creeping in, my body stiffening as I braced for the gauntlet of Seattle traffic and, beyond that, the limbo I'd wandered ever since that first MDMA session. I wanted more of *this*, the self-knowing and ease I felt here. But that felt a long way off.

I turned my attention back to my family's story instead. Was it a cop-out, an escape from an indistinct present? Maybe. Still, I couldn't escape the feeling I was venturing deep into uncharted territory, and that important information awaited me here.

14

Within a month from his "érettségi," the rigorous, comprehensive written and oral examinations which even today mark the end of a European secondary education, Muki had visited his family, passed his pre-induction physical, and was in the uniform of an officer candidate (Kadett) in Franz Joseph's Imperial and Royal Army: Black shako, brown tunic, black trousers, sword. He must have been very proud. Among other things, it marked his final, permanent passage from one class to another in that rigidly class-ruled, rank and title-conscious society of his day. He was trained as an artillery officer, as were the other graduates of real-gimnazia, and received the insignia of a second lieutenant (Faehnrich = Ensign) in the Spring of 1915.

Portland, August 2017: His dream of becoming a civil engineer dashed, my grandfather instead found himself in the midst of the first global war. Muki was sent to the Carnic Alps, the mountainous region north of Venice, above the easternmost cuff of Italy's boot. The killing and freezing and numbing bore-dom that would occur here was called "The White War." Back in Austria-Hungary, images of snow-topped mountains lent a sort of epochal glow to the conflict. But for the men doing the dirty work of soldiering, it was a different story. While Europe's armies were employing the most advanced killing machines yet conceived, their soldiers had regressed to using the most brutal of weapons—bayonets, daggers, clubs wrapped in barbed wire—to wrest control of sodden, mud-choked ditches from each other. Those defending higher ground rolled rocks and grenades down steep slopes at their attackers. In a scene ripped straight from *Monty Python,* one Austro-Hungarian unit reportedly hurled tin cans filled with their own excrement at the Italian *Alpini* below. One hopes *Faehnrich* Lorinczi was spared such a besmirching.

Most of what I'd learn about Muki's service came from books. And I learned a lot. I can tell you how brutal the war in the mountains was, how—unlike in the mud of the Western Front— the shell bursts of the projectiles my grandfather prepared sent splinters of rock scything through young men no different from him but for the color of their uniforms. I can describe how in-ept the leadership of the Imperial and Royal Austro-Hungarian Army was, how they deliberately mixed Hungarians with Poles, Austrians, Croats and others so as to quash sectarian urges. Instead the men, unable to understand even simple commands, were sent on headlong charges into enemy fire.

Still, it's all just history, written in the same pitiless black-and-white as the photos of those icy mountaintops. The mo-ment it changes for me, when the story reaches off the pages to seize me by the lapels, is the moment I click on an email sent from halfway across the world and a sheaf of images shuffles into my hard drive.

The email is from my cousin Antal. Antal is the son of Aunt Csupi, my father's sister. Csupi fled across the Austrian border after the Revolution of 1956, but Antal, just ten years old, stayed behind with Muki and Csurka. He's twenty-five years older than me, more like an uncle than a cousin. And the images he's sent—which I've never seen, or even imagined I *could* see—are of our young grandfather at war.

I'd reached out a few weeks before, asking if he could tell me anything about Muki's wartime service. Given that I'd essentially forgotten I had a Hungarian family at all, Antal was kind to scan the photos for me. Because his English isn't great, his son Pal, who's a few years younger than me, served as our intermediary. It was through Pal that I learned not only about the photos, but that Muki had taken many of them himself. In 1915, George Eastman's Kodak, the first practical consumer-grade camera, was roughly twenty-five years old. It was pricey but not pro-hibitive, and reliable enough to travel with.

As I clicked through the hi-res scans, another of those trap-doors opened inside me. The photos were beautiful: Tight, well-composed shots in antique sepia, the focus sharp enough to pick out establishing details. They're not images of combat, or even of struggle. If these are men at war they're also at ease, relaxing on a stone-strewn Alpine hill or seated at a wooden table set with many bottles of red wine and half-full tumblers. Smiling young men on a grand adventure, some of them lean-ing forward to make sure they're included in the frame. One of them, I realized, is my grandfather.

It required several minutes of intense concentration before I accepted it was really him. His features were soft and unfamil-iar: Eyebrows rising in a gentle arch, downturned mouth sug-gesting not displeasure but bemusement. Yet here he was, not just young but youthful. He was on an epochal adventure, and he looked more alive and present than in any memory of mine. He was one version of himself here, one that would fade over time. It's upon his shoulder that one of his fellow officer's hands rested so easily, and I found myself oddly charmed to know that others felt so warmly towards him. As I gazed at the photos of men whose names I'll never know, my grandfather suddenly seemed much closer, and also much further than ever before. In the blink of an eye, this handful of antique photographs had doubled my understanding of his life story.

That night, after dinner, I showed Julianna the photos. "Oh wow," she said. "These are incredible! They're really beautiful. Was this right before he was captured?"

"It must be within a couple of months, at most."

Julianna knew a little about Muki's journey herself. On a trip to Sicily, back in 2003, we'd visited one of its way posts: the picturesque fishing village of Cefalù.

Though it was only April, the Mediterranean sun was already blisteringly hot. We disembarked from a creaky railcar and wended our way towards the central *piazza*. As we strolled, I told her what little I knew about Muki's travails.

"So, in 1916 Muki was captured by the Italians, but I don't know how it happened. He was an artillery officer, so I doubt he was in a trench or on the front lines, but really, I'm just guessing."

I glanced longingly through the window of a café but it was closed for *riposto*, the Sicilian version of *siesta*. "Heck," said Julianna. "They really take nap time seriously here, don't they?" We resumed our walk, pausing to admire Cefalù's famous lagoon, the water so blue it looked artificial.

"Anyway, I do know this," I went on. "Muki ended up here, in Cefalù. My father told me that because he was an officer, he had it pretty easy. He was free to roam the town by day, so it was more like house arrest. His guards had to salute him, and he even had a manservant. And being a bookworm, he somehow got ahold of a some foreign-language volumes. By the time he was released in early 1919 he was fluent in Italian, French, and English."

By now we'd reached the *piazza*, a sun-bleached expanse of pale marble. I felt a stirring deep inside my chest. Muki must have stood here too, nearly a century before. My father had visited as well, some twenty years before now. I was enmeshed in an ancient dance: sons forever searching for their fathers. My father's words drifted back to me now: "If you ever visit Cefalù," he'd told me, "find the oldest-looking person you can, and ask for directions to the old police barracks. That's where Muki was held prisoner."

I looked around. There, across the weathered paving stones, was an elderly priest in a sun-bleached cassock. I approached him and choked out my question in skeletal Italian. He pondered for a moment, the faintest of smiles creasing his face, then pointed down a side street: "*Proseguire per due isolati e svoltare a destra.*" After a short walk, Julianna and I found ourselves in front of a flat-faced, unremarkable little building. I looked up at the sign: *Istituto Provinciale Linguistico.* My heart gave a little leap. By the poetry of chance, the former prison where my grandfather educated himself into a semblance of freedom was now a language school.

Now, as we sat around our kitchen table in Portland, I recalled the sense of wonder I'd felt back in Cefalù. It was Julianna's question that snapped me out of my reverie. "You told me he hated it there, right?" she said.

"Yeah. It's hard to believe in such a beautiful setting, but apparently he was really miserable. I actually looked up the origin of the word 'exile.' I didn't know this, but the Greeks, who founded Cefalù, reserved it for the most heinous of crimes. It was the worst punishment they had."

I paused for a moment. "My father didn't really say much about Muki as a person, or what he was like as a dad. But in his memoirs, he included this famous quote from the first days of World War I. It was from a British cabinet official, who said: 'The lamps are going out all over Europe. I don't think we shall see them lit again in our lifetime.' My father wrote that that's when the lamp of hope and ambition was extinguished in Muki, too."

"Your grandfather had PTSD," Julianna said. I was silent a long moment.

"I…I guess so. I never really thought about it that way. But yeah, that rings true. I do know this: Everything I know about him tells me that his life was pretty hard from the start, and it rarely got easier. Every time he seemed to have made it, the rug just got pulled out from under him."

In the days that followed, I felt a sadness sinking in, the faint but nagging suspicion that my grandfather had spent much of his life in quiet despair. I thought of the comfort and ease I'd enjoyed. My life had been so much easier than Muki's, and yet I'd rarely been truly happy. A better, more fulfilling place always beckoned from over the horizon, just beyond my grasp. Would I ever reach it?

A response, or something like it, arrived a week or so later. My phone rang one afternoon, and while I didn't recognize the number, something told me to take the call. "Hello," said an unfamiliar woman's voice. "I understand you're interested in attending a 'meditation circle' later this month. There's a spot for you, if you'd like it."

15

Portland, August 2017: I audibly gulped. Somehow, I'd forgotten all about Julianna's upcoming ayahuasca ceremony. Now, on the phone with this stranger—who with unsettling mysteriousness declined to provide her name—I felt pinned to the spot. Suddenly it seemed there was no escaping this confrontation with myself.

"So, ah…have you worked with psychedelics before?" the woman asked.

"Well, quite a lot when I was a teenager," I said with a nervous laugh. "But not really since then. I mean, wait, no: there was the MDMA therapy earlier this year."

"Ah…yeah. Sooo…" she trailed off for a moment. "An ayahuasca ceremony can be…challenging. We observe what's called… ah…noble silence. So, there's…no talking with anyone…except the facilitators."

"Um, okay. I can handle that."

"The…ah…suggested donation is…hmm…$300 per participant."

"Okay, got it."

As the conversation went on and the woman's tone became increasingly unfocused, I realized that I wasn't going to find the semblance of rigor I'd hoped for. This wasn't going to be like those MDMA sessions, where Julianna and I felt held inside a safe and clinical container. There would be no trained staff on hand, no nurses in case…in case of what? In case I threw up too violently? And yet I couldn't ignore the glow of excitement in my belly.

"Okay. I'm in."

The ceremony was only two weeks away. In the days leading up to it I felt an unfamiliar blend of emotions, a dawning curiosity mixing with cold dread. It made me feel like my guts were being squeezed from the inside out. Eventually, one blustery morning a few days before we were to sit, they broke open.

It was a weekday, while Evelyn was at school. Even now, I can't remember what set me off. Maybe I'd checked our dwindling bank balance and gone to unload on Julianna. Maybe she'd told me, for the thousandth time, that she wanted us to move. But as we stood face to face on the landing outside our bedroom, something cracked open and suddenly I was boiling over like an untended saucepan, wresting my stout wedding band off my finger and hurling it directly at her face. Most shocking of all, I heard my own voice saying: *"Why won't you let me be a man?"*

Fortunately, because I lack any athletic ability whatsoever, the ring didn't hit her. It flew past her and clanked to the bathroom floor instead. Even in our lowest moments, I'd never committed, or seriously considered, an act of physical aggression towards my wife. Now we stood staring at each other for a moment, wide-eyed and breathless. I literally had no idea why I'd said that.

"What…happened?" she asked. "Are you okay?"

"I…I just," I began. My throat felt tight. "I never feel like you actually want me. I'm more like your kid; you're more like my mother. And I'm sick of it. I'm so *sick* of it."

"Okay. I get it. Will you do something with me?"

"What?"

"Just come downstairs with me. To the basement."

As we descended the creaky old stairs, my chest felt like it was encased in cement. For all the liberation I'd felt in MDMA, I knew the medicine hadn't worked, that the magic wasn't for me. No one was coming to save me, and I was going to spend the rest of my life in this greyed-out purgatory.

I followed Julianna into the cool air of the rehearsal space, the one we no longer rehearsed in. She lit a votive candle she'd grabbed from her studio and then excused herself, returning a minute later with a blanket and a pillow. She laid me down on the cool floor, the candle throwing its dim flickers against the sound diffusers hanging from the walls. From the start of our relationship, Julianna's innate kindness had drawn me to her; now a hidden healer was revealing itself. Still, I felt numb under the soft press of the woolen blanket. The weight of what I'd said upstairs hit me now, and I closed my eyes in defeat.

"I don't know," I said. "I want to feel better, but I don't know how that can ever happen. I keep waking up and still being… me. It's so late, and I've wasted so much time."

Julianna listened in silence, her hand resting on my stomach. Finally she spoke.

"When we were upstairs, when you threw the ring. I know you were speaking to me, and I get it. This has been a shitty dynamic and I don't want to be your mom. But…who else were you speaking to?"

I was silent for a long moment. I thought back to the last years with Julianna, my sense of frustration and smallness. How charged sex felt, how my attraction to her was always subsumed by a slithery undercurrent of self-doubt. I was a middle-aged man, and yet sometimes I felt like I was eleven, my dawning sexuality forced deep underground by raw shame. An image rose in my mind's eye, as unwelcome as it was clear.

"That's easy," I finally said. "Irene."

16

Portland, August 2017: My mother Rhonda died in September of 1975. That Christmas, my father went to a holiday party in the Virginia suburbs. Entering the room, he was dumbstruck: There was Rhonda's double. Enter Irene.

The resemblance *was* striking, at least physically. Both women were tall, lean, darkly semitic. Both possessed a flair for the dramatic. But for all their external similarities—those patterned scarves and complicated hairstyles—they were very different women. If Rhonda walked with an essential surety, Irene's foothold was more tenuous. There was something unsettled and touchy about her, a need to be seen no seeing could appease. She and my father were married in May of 1976, eight months after my mother's death.

Now, in the cool darkness of the basement I felt back to that dark, nearly memoryless void, when all my landmarks had vanished overnight. "My father told me that after Rhonda died, his doctor gave him three sleeping pills," I told Julianna. "He enclosed my father's hand around the tablets with his own, and he said: '*You. Will. Get. Through. This*.'"

We were silent a long moment. My father did get through it, somehow, but that autumn a vast continent inside him slipped beneath the waves. My memories of those months are vestigial at best, but nowhere in them can I find my father. Already grief-stricken over Muki's death two months before, he plunged ever deeper into his work life, leaving my sister and me in Csurka's cold care. Some essential part of him winked out now, and it was as though I'd lost not one parent, but two. My father had determined to find a new mother for his children. Once Irene was on the scene, his job was complete.

"After Irene moved in, all the photos of my mother disappeared," I said. "It was as though she'd never even been there."

After a long moment, Julianna asked, very gently: "When did she start hitting you?"

I knew it was coming, and still I gave an involuntary squirm. "Jeez. I don't really know. It seemed pretty quick. Once she realized my father had no intention of slowing down his work life, it got ugly."

At this a reel of internal home movies spilled forth. I'm being slapped in the department store, where I'm taken on hateful shopping errands. Do the sales clerks turn away or nod in silent approval? Now I'm slapped in the parking lot below, the air pregnant with the odor of rain-slicked tires. Again in my house, on deep blue carpeting of the back stairs. But the film is jumbled and indistinct; I can't even tell if these memories are real. But I'll never forget looking up to see a dark shadow passing over my stepmother's face, the hard lines of her nose and jaw becoming something ancient and terrifying. I saw what I'd never been able to acknowledge: that my father had totally abandoned me to my fate.

"But look," I said. "We've had this conversation before. Irene could be loving and playful, too. Besides, everyone was hit by their parents in the '70s, weren't they? You were too."

"Yeah, but I don't know that it makes it any easier. I mean, can you imagine hitting our kid?"

I couldn't.

"I think what's different now is that you're being asked to just feel it. To acknowledge that it really happened, and to see what it implanted in you."

The cool weight of the air reminded me of our first home in Washington, how still and hermetic it felt. That house was built into the side of a hill, giving it a dark and fortress-like feel. It had always felt like it was protecting us from the outside world; now I saw how it concealed what went on inside, too. I was utterly powerless, and nobody was coming to save me. No one even knew it was happening.

But someone had. A sudden spark of memory, and then I was on my feet. "Can you wait here?" I trotted upstairs and came back with my laptop.

"Do you remember a few years ago, when my childhood neighbor looked me up? I pretty much forgot about it. Ah! Here it is." I began to read aloud:

> *My husband pointed out that I should have made it*
> *clear that I have not turned out A) divorced and now*
> *man-hungry, B) a violent felon (or any other type of*
> *felon, for that matter), or C) crazy stalker weird. My*
> *reason for looking for a childhood neighbor is because*
> *I have one memory, some thirty years old, that brings*
> *tears to my eyes now that I am a mother myself. And*
> *I need to know if it's accurate. And it's nothing wrong*
> *that any child did, so no worries on that account.*
> *So, the thing is, I remember you cutting your hair.*
> *And I remember exactly the shy, scared look on your*

face when you showed us, my Mom and me. You came out in that side yard, near the dogwood tree. And then my Mom was hurrying you into our kitchen where she tried to fix it as best she could, but it was pretty bad—there were almost bald patches in places. That night I came down after I was supposed to be asleep. I can't remember why. But I heard my Mom crying in the kitchen and so I crept. I was scared. My mom rarely cried. And my Dad was in there, too, and she was telling him, "She's just so horrid to him!" I remember "horrid" was the exact word she used, and I didn't know what it meant, but I knew it was bad. And my father was trying to console my Mom, telling her since she had fixed it, maybe it wouldn't be so bad. And I knew they were talking about you and about your stepmother.

I closed the screen. Julianna was silent. With only the candle for light, it was difficult to read her expression. "She saw what was happening," she finally said. "You didn't imagine it. It was real."

In my mind's eye, a great pile of puzzle pieces lay before me. My traumatized grandparents, my anguished mother, my rageful stepmother all jumbled together, and I had no idea how to begin putting them together. Now my father's image appeared before me. For all his native kindness, why hadn't he intervened?

The answers didn't come that day. But something the strange woman on the phone had said did. "When you're, ah…called to the medicine," she'd told me, "you may find it begins working with you…long before the ceremony."

It was only later that I realized how right she was. I'd begun keeping a journal a few months earlier, when things with Julianna were at their most fragile. Had I bothered to revisit it now I would've seen a vivid star chart wheeling above my head, a map as clear as the one laid out in my father's memoirs. Everything was leading me towards ayahuasca:

A massive evergreen under a yellow quarter moon.
Inside my chest: Gleams of blue and green light,
flecked with gold.
Deeper in my belly, a crimson glow.
Clearest of all: A thick and vine-like rope appearing
from out of the ground. Grabbing ahold, I'm dragged
all the way down into my core.

PART THREE

Medicine / Reunion

My mother, circa 1968

17

Portland, September 2017: "What the hell," I said, grunting under an armful of pillows and blankets. "Is this really the place?" As if Julianna would know. As we trudged up the steep driveway, what had appeared to be a single house revealed itself to be a complex: a cluster of structures hunching under a wooded slope. *A commune? The headquarters of a millenarian sex cult?* The only response was the quiet twittering of birds.

We'd only learned the address the day before: A quiet lane out in the Portland suburbs. *If anyone asks why you're here,* read the email, *tell them it's for a 'breath work session.'* Entering through a back door, we removed our shoes and stepped into a carpeted living room furnished with tasteful Buddhist-themed artwork. A handful of fellow-journeyers milled about or sat in anxious silence. Some were young people festooned with beads; one appeared to be a farmer, complete with a scraggly beard and grubby overalls. One or two had to be in their seventies. I wanted to ask them what was happening, but what was there to say? "Hi! Are we all about to die, or just lose our minds?" So I gazed out the window and tried to steady my racing heart.

Finally a young woman in clanking jewelry materialized from the kitchen. "Welcome," she said with a shy smile. "Please follow me downstairs."

The basement had all the charm of a freshman dorm. Inside a large and bare room, afternoon light filtered through tacked-up tapestries. Spread throughout the floor were twenty or so cushions with name tags. By each one, ominously, sat a plastic bucket. Julianna was stationed at the other end of the room from me. As we dispersed to our preassigned spots, I gave her hand a final squeeze.

At the head of the room, the facilitators—an older, slightly wizened man and a woman covered in tattoos of Sanskrit text—fussed over cups, candles, and sticks of incense. Now that everyone was gathered I noted, with a twinge of disappointment, that we were all Caucasians. Here we were, just a bunch of white people partaking of yet another resource plundered from the Amazon. I quietly swallowed the thought as, one by one, we rose from our blanket-lined nests, approached the altar, and accepted a cup of ominous, sludgy-looking brew to bring back to our seats. As I sat in nervous silence, long-buried memories of my teenaged journeys bubbled up. I'd felt at home in the psychedelic realms, wandering streets and alleyways shot through with ultraviolet light. What had I forgotten in the years since?

The hour it took to serve everyone in the room was a nerve-wracking eternity. When my turn to approach the altar finally arrived, I studied the facilitators' faces but they remained inscrutable. "Welcome," said the man, peering deep into my eyes. "What sized pour would you like?"

I hesitated a beat. "Um…large, I think." What point was there in taking half-steps now? I returned to my seat. The man gave a short blessing: "We drink to honor *Pachamama*—Mother Earth— and we ask for the wisest counsel, the truest knowing, and the loving support of this container."

We raised our cups and drank.

18

Portland, September 2017: At night, when I was young, a train would come for me. I'd sense the weight of iron wheels upon the tracks, hear the chuff of exhaust billowing from smokestacks too distant to see. But I felt it: The faint trembling of the windowpanes, the tricklings of pain inside my skull told me it was drawing closer by the minute. Soon I'd be helpless under its awful weight, the crush of ten thousand tons. Where could I go? There was no running from it, because I was the track.

The pain in my ear would spread, filling my entire head. There was even a color to it, a dull and sickly red like metal fresh from the forge. It was so close to my brain that it seemed less it was happening *to* me than it *was* me. I'd whimper in surrender, but there was no relief to be found. As the train approached my defenses would crumble. *Maybe it will be different this time*, I'd think. But it never was.

My father could not help me. My stepmother could not help me. Nothing could diminish the pain, not the chalky pink crunch of St. Joseph's aspirin, not the hot washcloths pressed against my head. On the nights the earaches came for me, time would bend, seeming even to fold backwards upon itself. Only the quiet metallic scrape of my bedside clock told me that morning and relief were coming. Eventually I'd wake up, surprised I'd dozed off. The only evidence of the previous night's storm was a yellow crust of dried pus crackling down my neck and a sensation of hollowness in my ear, as if something had been taken from me while I slept.

Pain is the symptom of being alive. I'm speaking medically here, not philosophically. Those who don't feel it—who suffer from genetic disorders such as congenital analgesia, for instance—aren't the lucky few, but a cursed minority. We need pain; it teaches us how to avoid danger and injury, how to stay alive. But pain doesn't always draw us together. No one else can feel our pain for us, and at its most abyssal depths it can feel as though we've regressed to the primordial state, lonely molecules abandoned to an unforgiving universe.

Those early experiences of pain traumatized me, but they gave me something in return: A new way to see. When the earaches came, my consciousness would extend out into the darkened landscape outside my bedroom window. Though my eyes were of little use here, I sensed the shadow-world around me was every bit as alive as the waking one, perhaps even more so.

Years later, I'd rediscover night through the electric lens of hallucinogens. Now I saw that darkness had been my natural home all along. I could move here; no interloper, but merely one of the thousand rightful animals of the dark. In my nocturnal rambles the earth seemed to breathe around and through me, the deep rumble of aspirations so palpable my whole body thrummed with them, a baby animal pressed to its mother's flank. When the earaches came these lysergic dreams were still years away. But I already sensed sound as a giver of life, the darkened world somehow more lawful and accepting than the day-lit one. I liked it here, held in this quiet symphony.

As I raised that first cup of ayahuasca to my lips, the memory of those long-ago nights arose unbidden. That and a very dim sense: That I was not leaving myself behind, but journeying to a place that had waited a long, long time for my return.

19

Portland, September 2017: I have tasted many odd and unpleasant things in my life. In northern Japan, a dried sea squirt: Gnarled and bitter as a padlock. At a backyard barbecue here in

Portland, a roasted pig's eye: Wet and livery, the crunchy lens embedded in goo. But they have nothing on ayahuasca.

After I'd choked down the contents of my cup with a shudder and felt reasonably sure I'd hold the viscous goop down—for the moment, at least—I settled back into my nest of blankets and waited to see what would happen next. My thoughts ping-ponged between worry the medicine simply wouldn't work, as Renee had warned might happen, and fear that it *would*, in ways I couldn't control. But as the daylight peeking through the tacked-up blankets drained from the room, the faintest of waves began to animate my body. Like it or not, something was indeed happening.

As if on cue, the female facilitator begins to sing: A lovely and supple soprano, weaving an hypnotic incantation through the air. Later, I'd learn she was singing an *icaro*, or "magic song." We are thousands of miles from the Amazon, merely a bunch of white people sitting in a suburban basement. And yet as the song wends its way into and through me, my skepticism begins to dissolve.

A subtle tingling animates my extremities, a rising vibration seeking out vestiges of trauma. First my ankles, broken in a motorcycle accident nearly thirty years before, then the nearly invisible pair of scars just above my waist. I realize with quiet shock it's been years since I even noticed them. They're small and easy to miss (and I *am* somewhat furry) but what arises now is the sense of shame around these incisions, evidence of an adolescent surgery to correct incompletely descended testicles. I remember being told the operation was for a "hernia," a term that was never convincingly explained. The distaste my family attached to the body, especially the organs of sex, feels suddenly palpable and close. *What else did they do to me?*

The rush of sensations ramps up, queasy waves of energy sloshing through me. My mind starts to race, desperate to quantify what's happening. But it's far too fast, and far too powerful. Closing my eyes, I'm dragged into a vast temple built into the earth, the realm of a boundless intelligence. I'm in the presence of some awe-inspiring sentience, less a single being than the sum of all possible beings. Equal parts terrified and thrilled, I choke out a soundless challenge: *What are you trying to tell me? Show me!* But if anyone or anything is listening, it remains silent.

I descend deeper into a world of darkness and indistinct shapes. I realize I'm inside the tunnel of fibrous roots and rock-choked earth, the one I'd written about in my journal. Fractal patterns rise up, seizing my attention before quickly fading away. Halls of pale light form, a geometric grid of electricity unrolling into an endlessly vanishing horizon. Grabbing ahold, I'm pulled at unfathomable speed for a few moments, only to be dropped back into the landscape dissolving and recreating itself below me.

Very far below me, my body writhes on a blanket. This isn't right. Everything is moving far too quickly and also too hot, too cold, too slow. My mind can't make sense of this place and suddenly I feel a sadness that is nearly bottomless. I have failed a crucial test. *This was your only chance.*

Now I understand what I'd hoped would happen. Like those MDMA journeys—which by the way are feeling a *fuck of a lot* kinder and safer than this nightmare—all I wanted was to drink the potion and be cured. But I'm not. Desperation truly takes hold of me now, the yawning fear that I'll never escape my thoughts. I am sinking into utter darkness, and I have never felt more lost.

20

Portland, September 2017: Eventually it was determined that my faulty ears required surgery. Tiny culverts were inserted into my eustachian tubes, the tunnels leading from the middle ear to the top of the throat, to enable them to drain. A safe and minor operation, though it hadn't always been so. I was surprised to learn that the first recorded myringotomy, as it's known, was performed in 1649. For the first few centuries the procedure had an iffy safety record as physicians inserted tubes and grommets of various materials—rubber, gold foil, whale bone—with varying degrees of success. With the introduction of vinyl tubes, in 1954, myringotomies finally became routine and predictable. Between the ages of five and eight I'd undergo three of them.

These operations opened more than just my blocked eustachian tubes. The first time the anesthesiologist held the rubber mask over my face, a strange thing happened. Clawing through a wave of nausea—it was as if all the oxygen in the room had been replaced by rubber cement fumes—my vision morphed. The asbestos ceiling tiles above me began to slide of their own accord, a self-generating Tetris clicking into puzzling new arrangements. The anesthesiologist's eyes, the only part of his face I could see above his teal-green mask, took on an eerie intensity. In the instant before nothingness took me, a thought rose up: *What if this was how things really were?*

My time in this fluid environment was fleeting, a scene glimpsed from the window of a high-speed train. As quickly as it came on I was in the recovery room, wondering where I'd gone. Even after the anesthesia faded, the question remained. I'd always felt the dim sense there was something behind what I ordinarily saw. Now I had proof.

21

Portland, September 2017: In the endless ayahuasca basement, time slows to the thrum of a giant's heartbeat. My struggles are getting me nowhere. I'm not panicking exactly, not run-out-of-the-room screaming. (I can neither run nor scream right now.) But as the geometric visions fade, a shape materializes before me, a towering obsidian wall. Above its lip, hundreds of feet above me, I can make out the faintest scrim of stars. This can't be anywhere on Earth, or even this galaxy. The recognition hits me a moment later, and as it does my heart sinks like a stone. I've been here before, though it's been decades. I've returned to the Barrier.

I first encountered the Barrier on my LSD-fueled teenage rambles. It's an impenetrable screen, a great circular wall enclosing me. I'm transfixed by the blue and green webs of electricity pulsing over it before I realize this may actually be from an episode of *Star Trek* ("The Tholian Web") in which aliens build a space net to capture the *Enterprise.*

Some part of me knows the Barrier isn't real, but that doesn't diminish my sorrow. I've squandered so much time since then, and for what? Fifteen precious years dripped by as I dawdled in self-protective slumber, and now I'm right back where I started. If I ever required an excuse to end my own life, surely this is it. *This was your only chance,* the Voice whispers. I feel paralyzed by grief.

Now it's Julianna's voice I hear inside me, though she's on the other end of the room, lying still on her nest of blankets. She's urging me to remain here, not to wriggle out from it. *You think you can't survive this, but you* are *surviving it,* she says. *Just stay. Just stay and feel it.*

What would happen if I surrendered? If I accepted I *have* been here before, and that I've returned for a reason. Here, finally, is the truth: I don't know how to find my way out of this maze, and I'm asking for help. Maybe my mind—the thing I thought was me—can't help. Maybe it wants relief from this endless dance, too. And with this I feel the faintest stirrings of hope.

My writhing ceases and I lie still, an insect pinned by the thumb of the cosmos. I have never quite submitted so utterly and prayerfully. As desperate as I felt a moment ago, I see now there is nothing to fix, to do, to manage. I am not in charge, and I never have been. My nature isn't my fault—*or even a fault at all*—but the lawful result of my genetics, my upbringing, the stories that told me who I was. As I let this knowing percolate through me I feel a gratitude that's nearly shocking in its totality. In response my belly begins to roil, and I know what must happen next. Even within the gut-wrenching, horrific eruptions now racing to exit my body there is deep medicine at work. This mortifying submission feels, of all things, like an act of devotion. Maybe even a prayer. I'm so grateful I said yes.

Exhausted, I kneel back into my nest, or I try to. Of its own accord, my body is bowing deeply and repeatedly to the altar at the head of the room, a strand of kelp caught in the cosmic stream. I bow to the medicine, to the facilitators, to the music working its way through my blood like oxygen. The songs are unfamiliar, the farthest thing from the dark and aggressive music I've always gravitated towards. The Amazonian *icaros*, the Indian *kirtans*, even the more modern and polished spiritual songs all penetrate me in ways I wouldn't have thought possible only a few hours before.

Well, almost. As the facilitator fiddles with his iPhone and pulls up a prerecorded track, I know there aren't enough drugs in the world to make me love the Native American chant superimposed over a plodding dance floor beat.

Clutching my purge bucket, I gingerly stand and pick my way through the darkened room. Ascending the staircase, I feel like an electron transiting the circuits of some vast brain. When I pass other journeyers we are glowing wraiths treading luminous paths. We are utterly and flawlessly beautiful here.

22

Portland, September 2017: It's silent and dark upstairs; I'm alone. Outside, shadows play across the sprawling wooded yard. *I'd like to walk around out there*, I think, *but then I might not come back.* I stay inside.

Maybe it's the medicine's pull, but this place feels familiar. The dated kitchen and the overstuffed armchairs remind me of the house my family moved to in 1986, when Irene could no longer stand to dwell in Rhonda's domain. I loathed this house as much as I'd loved the one we'd left. The old house was secretive and knowing; this one was showy and grandiose. Irene ran rampant here, replacing Rhonda's mod furnishings with new ones in ambivalent pastels. I moved out two years later, at the age of seventeen. The place was less a faded memory than no memory at all, a two-year void in the record.

I lie down on the floor and gaze up at the ceiling. As soon as I feel the pleasurable grind on carpeting on my back, other recollections rise up. Like those slender scars below my belly, I've so thoroughly forgotten them that, for a long moment, I'm not sure if I'm making it up: The year I spent with heroin.

I was nineteen or twenty. I can't remember. Unlike nearly everyone else in my high school class, I didn't go to college, didn't even bother to apply. The path my father had worked so hard to lay out before me—multiple degrees, a bustling legal or medical practice—felt meaningless. I saw no place for myself in *that* world, the one lit by the sun. And so I entered the nighttime one, where I worked in grubby nightclubs and second-hand bookstores, lived in trashy punk houses and slept til midday. When I wasn't onstage, electricity leaping off the strings of my bass guitar, I barely felt alive.

My high school bandmates, like most of the people I knew, had gone off to college. Directionless, I could only think to get more lost. In the Washington, D.C. of the early '90s, hard drugs weren't hard to find. And though a steady drumbeat of fatal ODs coursed through the scene, I wanted to lose myself, and I wanted it now. So I began injecting.

I loved the ritual and the secrecy, the irresistible pull of the drug that dissolved me into nothingness. I reveled in my wretchedness, the reverberations of all those childhood slaps across my face. I loved heroin's power, the rollercoaster plunge as it crushed me under its landslide, somehow removing all sensation even as it allowed me to feel something—*anything*—in my nerve-dead body. Limbs dissolving into goo, heartbeat slurred and indistinct. The boy whose own mother had given up on him, I faded into the nothingness I knew I deserved.

Every weekend or so I bought a bag and by Monday it was gone. But I never became addicted. After a year, I stopped. I don't know why, whether it was the promise of a new band or a new girlfriend or any of the other things I hung on to convince myself I was somehow on the right course, that there was any kind of course to be on.

The simple touch of carpeting brings all this rushing back in a blur, an entire wasted year I'd forgotten. Dazed, I rise to my feet to peer out the window to the darkened landscape. Shadows dance through the foliage, falling across the trunk of a massive Douglas fir. It's releasing a nearly audible sigh with each of its respirations.

This memory is so foreign it feels like a dream. Who was I then? But even within heroin's spell some quiet voice had sustained me, refusing to fully wink out. I'd heard it again after the first MDMA session, when self-acceptance felt like the most fragile of seedlings. Now, in ayahuasca's gentle grip, it feels as unshakable as the evergreen towering over the house. I'm being asked to return to myself. And this time, I know I can't refuse.

I sense it's time to rejoin the group, but something tells me to pause just a moment longer. I absently stroke my temples with featherlight fingertips, something I can't recall ever doing before. This touch awakens something, a reminder of a time before time, before the imprint of those movie-memories. My mother must have done the very same thing when I was young, before we lost each other. Now, as if summoned up from a deep well, the image of her face arises before my own.

I stand perfectly still, transfixed as we gaze at each other. I remember visiting the cemetery to inter my father's ashes twenty years before, the shock of seeing her name inscribed on the columbarium next to his. Before that moment, I had never for an instant believed there was any evidence of her passage here on this earth.

I long to talk with her, to know what her voice sounds like. But she doesn't say a word. She just gazes at me from beneath that dark wave of hair. More than anything, I sense that her spirit isn't separate from mine but resides inside me, where it's always been. It's never even occurred to me to look.

23

Portland, September 2017: I go back downstairs to rejoin the ceremony. Earlier, caught in the gears of the medicine, I felt like some cosmic plaything, tossed like a pebble in surf. Now I feel borne on sound: A silvery, enveloping shimmer like the tone that filled the apartment after my father's death. It has waited for me all this time.

It's time for a second pour of the medicine, for those who desire it. A cluster of fellow journeyers kneel before the altar and I join them without hesitation, knocking back the thick brew with a shudder and crawling back to my nest. Julianna is sitting up now. As if signaling her inner state, her hair has exploded into a halo that's somehow both comical and beautiful. As I pass her I shoot her a queasy smile. She returns it, mouthing a silent "Wow." I know I'll be returning here, to the next ceremony, and the one after that. How could I not? It occurs to me that this might also be a textbook description of "drug addiction." But strange though this night has been, I feel an incontrovertible rightness. I recognize that my body knows, and with this I gently shush my critical mind. My limbs are growing heavy, and I know it's time to lie down again.

Back in my rumpled nest, where I've lost the ability to operate my blankets and pillows, the journey begins again. As the electric candles at the altar throw their flickers around the room, the older man facilitating the ceremony rises to dance amidst the shadow play. His silhouette is a cave painting come to life, and I'm certain I've never seen anything quite so eerie and beautiful.

As the medicine takes hold I feel myself dragged underground again, into an ocean constructed not of water but of roots, rocks, and dirt. Now every animal in creation arises to pass through me: Stampedes of insects, snakes, rabbits, wild boar and jaguar following in endless chase as I descend further and further into memory, into history, into the dark dreamscape of the earth and of my family. But what seizes me is not the relief of the medicine and the warmth of its electromagnetic waves. What comes now is fear, the memory of the deep dread I felt as a young child at bedtime.

Every evening after my stepmother dimmed the bulb of my blown-glass lamp, the stories I'd absorbed in daylight—the ones gleaned from the war books lining the walls of our house—would spring to life. I knew the soldiers were coming, and though I never saw them, the wetness of their breath and the threat of their touch were a nearly sexual presence surrounding my pre-pubescent body. I'd never connected these dreads before, how badly those images of atrocities had corroded my ability to be intimate.

Now, in the ayahuasca basement, I feel myself sinking. An hour before I thought I'd plumbed the limits of my despair; now I recognize this was only a prologue. Fear is woven so deep within my body that I've never recognized it as an alien voice. I've lived my entire life afraid, and the possibility of changing feels absurd. And so I do something I've never done before, never believed I could or would do: I begin to pray.

Please, Spirit.... I'm trying my best but I can't do this alone. I feel like I've wasted my life and I don't know how to make it right. Please help me. For Julianna, for our daughter, for myself.

After a time, something relents. My breath deepens, my heart stops thumping so hard. What comes now, a viscous liquid working through me, cell by exhausted cell, is forgiveness. I've spent so many years believing I was broken. Some part of me always believed that Rhonda's death and Irene's abuse had knocked me off my true path: *A doctor! A lawyer! A senator!* Now, held in this quiet grace there is nothing to fix, nothing to apologize for, nothing to undo. I am, for the first time I can remember, truly all right.

Held in this pale afterglow, I see that ayahuasca won't heal me, not by itself. That's my job. There is no choice but to take what I've been shown and put it into action. My eyes aglow with the wild fire of the initiate, I know, for the very first time, that I'm going to make it.

24

Portland, September 2017: "What...happened?" asked Julianna. "Did I just vomit up my demons?" In the pale glow of the instrument panel, her face looked ghostly and wan. I was silent, keeping my focus on the darkened road. "I don't know," I finally said. "But...I think everything is different now."

After the ceremony had closed, we'd all brought forth bowls of fresh fruit and nuts to share. As the room filled with happy chatter, I surveyed the scene in exhausted wonder. Many of us had wrestled with traumas that far outstripped any of mine. And though we'd all observed the prescription to observe "noble silence" during the ceremony, as each of us shared our experiences it was clear we'd all felt the support of the group as we descended into the unknown. Even in darkness, we were not alone.

Now, in the car, I struggled to orient myself in this altered landscape. "Is this what the bends feel like?" I asked. "I mean, do we even have regular lives anymore?" Julianna was silent, but as the medicine gently relinquished its grip she reached out and held my arm for the remainder of the drive home.

"I...I felt what it would be like to be big," said Julianna. "Not hiding myself anymore, not hiding my art. I was with this forbidden part of me that's really ambitious. It's felt so uncomfortable my whole life; it's never been allowed. I guess they don't call it 'shadow' for nothing."

"When I met you, you would sometimes cover your mouth when you spoke. Do you remember? I'd pull your hand away. It's tender to remember."

"I know; it's tender for me, too. But I can love that young part of me—I have to. It was just a stage I had to pass through; I was always being told I was too much. So much shame."

Later, as we lay in bed entwined in a tangle of limbs, a feeling remained: That I was returning to myself. I saw with merciful clarity the discordances in my life, the way I hid out in my basement, buying more audio gear so as to ignore my essential failure to launch. And I saw, with intermingled sadness and acceptance, how I'd kept Evelyn at arm's length with endless correctives and reprimands, replaying the same style of conditional love I'd been shown.

Ayahuasca hadn't fed me my lines or told me what to do. It hadn't fixed me. But a moment from the end of the ceremony flashed back to me. As the medicine gently relinquished its hold, it brought me back to The Barrier one last time. The vast wall was as impenetrable as ever, but some inner voice told me to try something I never had before: to reach out and touch its great stone flank. I practically gasped in surprise: My fingers passed right through it. The Barrier wasn't real, and it never had been.

Most of all, I felt the depth of my bond with Julianna. We'd vaulted a crevasse together, and we'd had to depend on each other. I sensed a new capacity coming online in me, the quiet *clicks* of long-dead circuits firing back to life. It'd been so long since I'd trusted my intuition I'd stopped believing it was even possible. I felt, for the first time I could recall, a deep and utterly unshakable sense of self-acceptance.

There was one more thing. As much as this night had been focused on my own struggles, I'd heard the faintest of murmurs in the middle distance, a soft Hungarian voice that sounded eerily like my grandmother Csurka's. If reconnecting with my father's memoirs had shown me a hidden map, ayahuasca's ultraviolet light had revealed its hidden byways. Now, as my fingers scrabbled in the roots of ancestral memory, I felt a quickening. As Julianna and I dropped into fitful slumber, a whisper punctuated my sleep. *Look to the east*, it said. Back to the city of my father's birth, to the place that had both made and broken him. To Budapest.

PART FOUR

Disintegration

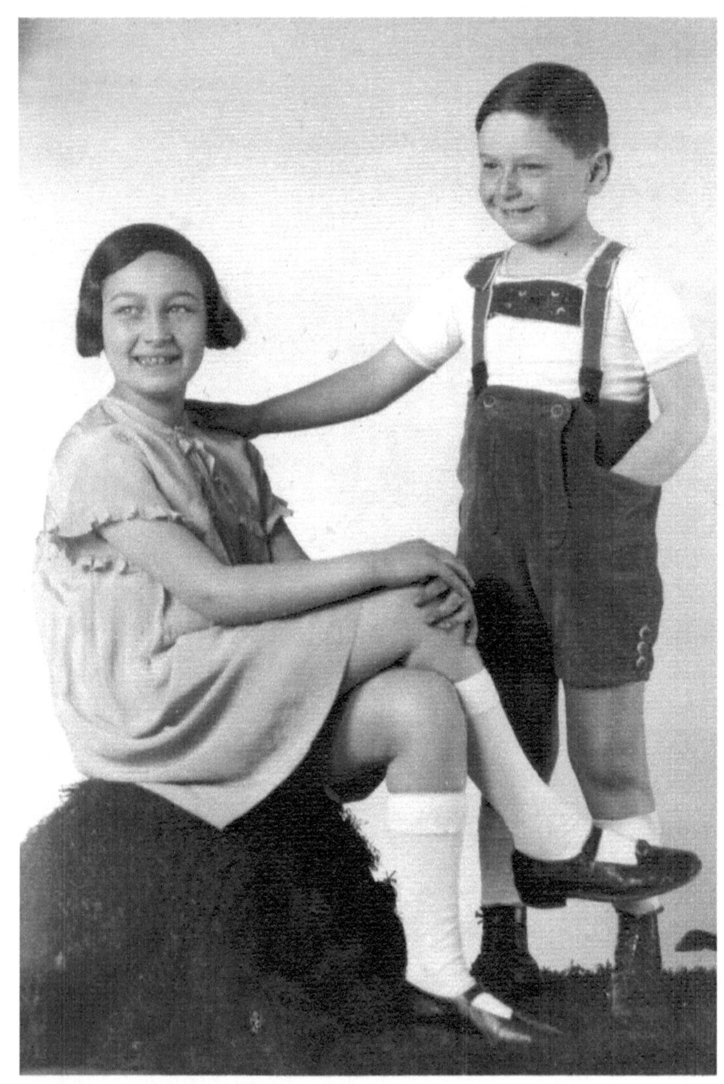

My father (right) and his sister, Aunt Csupi, circa 1935

25

Portland, September 2017: The next morning, nothing had changed. The sunlight streaming through the blinds, the features of the bedroom, Julianna's comforting shape stirring beside me; they were all in their proper place. My vision wasn't split by flashbacks or trails; I didn't hear ominous voices inside my head. In fact, I felt impossibly sober. But everything was different, and for a long moment it was all I could do to sit still, breathe slowly, and take it all in. As eerie as last night's visions had been, what persisted now was an essential sense of rightness. As far out as I'd gone, what I'd seen and felt was as true in the light as it'd been in the dark of the night before. There was no going back.

Julianna stretched and yawned beside me. As she opened her eyes we stared at each other in mock horror before we both burst out giggling. "What the *hell*," I asked, "was *that*?"

"Beats me. How long did we sleep? We need to pick up Evelyn from my mom's at noon."

"I'm guessing five hours?" As I picked up my phone to check the time—*yup, five hours on the dot*—I saw that my cousin Deborah had called.

This was unusual. For one thing, it was only recently that we'd been in touch at all; in the years following my father's death we'd barely spoken. When we did, tiny land mines would erupt without warning: Memories of the brunch in which I'd let fly a painful barb, the dinner party soured by one of her temper tantrums. Try as I might, I couldn't let down my guard or forget how punishing our time in Florida had been.

But ever since MDMA, I'd felt a welcome thaw. We began to schedule monthly telephone calls, and as her warmth came flooding back in, I found myself relaxing. But today wasn't our day to talk. What's more, I saw she'd called several times. She'd left a single voicemail, her voice wracked by sobs. "Call me as soon as you get this," she said. "Something terrible has happened."

26

Portland, September 2017: I pulled on some clothes and walked outside. The backyard was sun-dappled and quiet; juncos and chickadees flitted between stalks of mullein. I inhaled deeply and pulled up Deborah's number. It was her husband Isai's image that flashed through my mind: devilish beard framing a timeless face, his bright and mischievous eyes. Isai and his eleven-year-old son had arrived as refugees from Ukraine in the mid-'90s, after men on a pogrom—*yes, they still happen there*—broke into their apartment and beat them unconscious. I knew Isai was thirteen years Deborah's senior, and she eighteen years mine. I hadn't expected him to live forever but still, I'd have put even odds on his outliving her.

When Deborah picked up, her voice was unsteady.

"Hi darling," she began. "This…this morning, I was awakened by the dogs barking to be let out. Isai gets up early, but I didn't see him. I opened the door to his bedroom, and…" Now she broke down completely. "He was slumped against the headboard…his skin was white; the mattress beneath him was soaked in blood. The gun was lying on the floor."

I stood there, stunned.

"Oh, the coroner's here. I have to go."

"Okay, I love you. I'll call you this evening."

As I walked back into the house, my legs felt unsteady. For months I'd felt our monthly talks drawing Deborah and me closer; now I felt the awfulness of what she'd told me bearing down on me. Isai's face arose before mine again. Wanting a fresh start, he and Deborah had only recently moved from Vermont to Laramie. The awful gravity of his act tugged at me. What shadow part of him demanded his own annihilation?

That night, as Julianna, Evelyn and I gathered at the dinner table, I wondered what to say. Since that first MDMA session, we'd taken to saying grace before our meals. It was my turn to speak tonight but I faltered, suddenly tongue-tied. Evelyn hadn't seen Isai since she was an infant; she probably didn't even remember him. Surely I could wait a little longer—*or forever*—to tell her what he'd done. I exhaled and began to speak.

"I'm so grateful for this food, for my family…." I began. "And I want to send extra love to my cousin Deborah. She's in a lot of pain and needs our support."

Evelyn turned to face me. "Why? What happened?"

I thought back to what I'd been told, and not told, after my mother died.

"Isai died this morning…."

Her eyes widened: *"What? How?!?"*

I floundered for a moment, then went on: "He decided to end his own life. I think he was just feeling…done."

Evelyn was silent, her face distant and unreadable. Then she looked directly at me: "Are you going to do that?"

For a long moment, I froze. I'd never put a gun to my head, never stepped into the bathtub with a razor blade in my hand. What had she seen in me that I hadn't? Once again, Isai's image burned painfully bright inside me. I believed that suicide was an option I'd closed the door on forever. But really, I didn't know, just like I hadn't really known Isai. I answered as truthfully as I could: "I don't intend to."

Evelyn turned back to her dinner.

I talked to Deborah once more that day. I'd worried this loss might destroy her, but hearing her quiet calm, my fears receded a bit. The weight of what had happened was palpable and thick, but she was also startlingly, beautifully present.

"I know this was what he wanted, and I know he loved me completely," she began. "It's okay, in its own awful way. It just... is. He absolutely did not do this to hurt me. The hardest thing in my life was losing your mother. I'm stronger now; if I could take that, I can take this. I wanted so much to take that pain off of you, but there was no way I could...."

Now she cried in earnest. I sensed my own tears pressing against the dam behind my eyes, felt myself clench against them and then—gently, quietly—I set them free.

My cousin and I sat in silence for a long moment, me in my darkened living room, she in her house, suddenly alone. Now it was marked by Isai's passing, the bullet lodged above the ceiling. Perhaps someone would find it one day and know.

"Your daughter is so strong and so fierce, she can hold this," she said through her tears. "She has to learn what this sadness is, and know it doesn't have to own her. This ends here."

I knew she was right, and I breathed a quiet sigh of relief. I told her I wanted to come see her, and soon. "Let's convene in a couple of months, around my birthday," she said, "once I've settled Isai's affairs and done some processing."

As soon as we said our goodbyes and hung up, I bought a plane ticket.

27

Portland, October 2017: In the following days, Evelyn's question continued to ping inside me. I thought I'd done a good job of hiding my bouts of angst from her; now I wasn't so sure. I thought about what my father had written about Muki, how the "lamp of hope" had been extinguished. And I turned back to his memoirs, hoping to learn more.

Muki returned to Budapest from Sicily in 1919, one of thousands of former POWs streaming back home. Hungary had changed. The majestic boulevards and fantastical *Art Nouveau* mansions were all the same; it was the people who had morphed, or only revealed what had lain dormant. As the country writhed under wartime deprivations and the Army's ineptitude became clear, coded messages began to appear in newspaper editorials, spouted from the mouths of opportunistic politicians. *Perhaps Hungary had become infected by some unpatriotic pathogen; might there be certain social elements whose loyalties lay elsewhere?* Scandals involving the sale of shoddy equipment to the military stoked resentment against Jewish-owned provisioners. It was well-known, remarked Baron Gyula Madarassy-Beck, a financier and member of Parliament, that behind any bank one could always find "the Jew."

This was the home to which Muki returned. He'd surmounted his peasant upbringing, served his emperor in a punishing theater of battle, spent nearly three years as a prisoner of war. But as he stepped off the train wearing his first lieutenant's uniform and his army's second-highest combat decoration, it was his face that gave him away. Muki's feet had barely touched the platform before a passer-by spat *"Piszkos zsidó"* at him: *Dirty Jew.*

I shook my head in wonder. Even before ayahuasca, Muki's story had entranced me. My quiet and inward grandfather became someone else: An actor in a bracing and cinematic saga sweeping across endless grasslands, ancient cobblestoned streets, icy mountain peaks. Now things were about to get dramatic in a very different way; I doubt he could have imagined just how bad it could get.

At the close of the war, the Austro-Hungarian Empire had come apart like a chunk of rotted wood, plunging Hungary into a power vacuum. Simultaneously, a wall of death appeared on the horizon: the global influenza pandemic. Public life ground to a standstill; schools, churches, railways, and public facilities all shuttered their doors as the disease swept through in an invisible wave. By the close of 1918, roughly thirty Budapesters were dying from influenza every day.

Hungary's troubles had hardly begun. Now the country was whipsawed by two revolutions within a six-month span. The first kicked off with the prime minister being shot to death in front of his family. The next was a communist revolution inspired by the Soviet model. It hung on for a few disastrous months before a foreign invasion, including troops from Hungary's arch-nemesis Romania, sent the Bolsheviks packing. Now the National Assembly called square-jawed Admiral Miklos Horthy, an aristocratic war hero, out of retirement to serve as Hungary's regent. Thus began the "White Terror," a two-year campaign of state-sponsored violence against supporters of the previous regime. Ominously, many were Jews, drawn to communism as a way to negate their semitic roots. Instead, they'd planted the seeds of a hideous retribution.

For the most part, the death squads targeted small towns like Orgovány, where one night in late 1919 a band of armed men took entire families—three dozen souls in all—into the dark woods outside town, never to be seen again. But at the Kelenföld army barracks, just two miles from Inner Pest, drunken soldiers were committing unspeakable acts against entire families, games of sexual humiliation ending with corpses dumped in the Danube, men with the evidence of their manhood crushed beyond recognition, sometimes excised completely.

For Muki there was a single ray of hope. Amid the throngs of veterans desperate for work, my grandfather, thanks to the language skills he'd picked up in Cefalù, managed to find a job as a clerk at the General Credit Bank in Pest. One day he noticed a shy and modest young woman seated behind a secretary's desk. Unlike him, she had a benefactor: Her Uncle Desző—the guy in the oil painting Deborah and I squabbled over after my father died—was a rising star at the bank. Muki and Csurka were married in 1923. Two years later came a daughter, my Aunt Csupi. And in 1929 came a son, my father. Lorinczi György Gábor in the Hungarian idiom, George Gabriel Lorinczi in ours.

I'd never really pondered the world my father was born into. Not that he'd shared a great deal: mostly sepia-toned stories of family vacations, where tables groaned under the weight of roast goose, my grandmother's famous *rácz*-style carp baked in a tart tomato and sour cream sauce, sweet plum dumplings for dessert. Unlike those tall tales about commanding a tank in Korea, I didn't doubt these stories were true. But now I saw that they weren't the whole truth. My father had hidden much of our backstory from me, and I'd never understood why. Now I had an inkling, and with this the past and the present came together with a near-audible *click*.

From the disgrace of my grandfather's peasant upbringing to the sorrow that defined my grandmother's adolescence, my family had rarely enjoyed the sustained experience of ease. The World War had shattered something essential in Muki, taken the life of Csurka's first love. Even after the fighting was over, Hungary was subsumed in political unrest, mass violence, a rising tide of hate. It was Hungary, not Germany, who enacted the continent's first antisemitic law of the modern age, the "Numerus Clausus" act of 1920 restricting Jewish university admissions.

Searching online one afternoon, I stumbled upon an archive of antisemitic propaganda from this time, including broadsheets depicting hook-nosed, weak-chinned Jews. From the early '20s they began to appear everywhere, plastered on billboards and tacked to the round news posts that still dot the streets of Budapest. Even before he was able to read, my father must have seen these caricatures and understood how Hungary felt about Jews like him. Tiny memory bubbles of my own burbled up: the way my father avoided crowds and mass events, how he tried—and failed—to mix with the rugged, football-tossing dads of my childhood neighborhood. Even the way he spoke, his American English betraying no regional accent whatsoever. There was something shadowy and indistinct about the way he carried himself, and what was strangest was that I was the only one who saw it. No one else seemed to notice.

Suddenly, I knew what I had to do. I had to write a book about it all.

It didn't make any sense. I hadn't written anything in years, certainly nothing personal. I needed to drum up some work, not drop deeper into some historical rabbit hole. And yet the idea wouldn't let me go. Since ayahuasca I'd had the sense I'd stepped into a new arena, some liminal space where the answers I sought—*what exactly was I doing with my life? why had I never really felt like I belonged to anything?*—were far closer than I suspected.

But where? I'd been digging through my family story every possible way, or so I'd thought: poring through my father's recollections and obscure history books, listening for clues in the eerie byways of ayahuasca. And yet all this time there'd been a living, breathing source of information at my very fingertips. All that was required was for me to pick up the phone.

The next morning I flipped open my father's old leather-bound address book, searching for a telephone number in Switzerland.

28

Portland, October 2017: "Oh, Seth! What a wonderful experience to hear your voice! I'm in an old people's home. It's horrible, and I'm waiting for death!"

The moment I heard Aunt Csupi's cultured Hungarian accent, a puzzle piece clicked into place. At ninety-two, my aunt is the last living connection to a world that seemingly winked out decades ago. Inside me the door to an airship-sized hangar swung open, slim shafts of sunlight piercing halos of dust.

"Aunt Csupi! I'm so glad I reached you. The receptionist doesn't speak English, and I was worried I wouldn't be able to get through."

"Well, they are very stupid here. So! My darling Seth, how are you?"

It's been years since we've spoken, and I'm grateful she's chosen not to make an issue of it. I could've picked up the phone anytime, but Csupi is…well, complicated. Haughty and imperious, prone to outrageous proclamations, she seems to love nothing more than slinging righteous scorn. She once engaged in a years-long feud with her upstairs neighbors. I'm not sure, but it may have started when she called the police *on her own party* to compel the guests to leave.

Then there's the issue of racism. I sometimes describe Csupi as a Jew who survived the Holocaust to become a Nazi. It's an exaggeration, but not by much. Her monologues are peppered with caustic asides about Muslims, Catholics, Jews, members of our family, anyone and anything she finds objectionable. Which, it turns out, is pretty much everyone. Once, describing a trip to North Africa in a letter to me, Csupi actually wrote:

> *"...Even though they were Arabs, the men were polite and helpful, not like in Europe where all of the men are HOMOS."*

After a few minutes of chitchat, I gently cracked open the door. In his memoirs, my father wrote that the first thing Muki and Csurka did after marrying was to move across the river from Pest to a dowdy apartment block in Buda, at #2 Szász Károly Street. What he hadn't noted was the implicit messaging behind it. Pest was the city's more Jewish side; moving to Buda was a quiet signal, a sloughing off of old skin.

"So, Csupi," I said, "my father never told me much about growing up. What was life like on Szász Károly?"

"Well, it was a fine place to grow up. But a very strict environment in our apartment. We weren't allowed to have a radio or a phonograph; Muki believed they were only for lazy people."

"What about Csurka?"

"She was an angel! But always very melancholy. She didn't like to talk about the past. And there were her heart troubles. She was very discreet, of course. But even before the war she had angina and heart attacks. She was in the hospital three times; I thought she was going to die. The same with your father."

"Right! His ear infections." I flipped through my father's memoirs to where he'd written about them himself:

> *The pain came soon enough. At about age three I somehow caught an ear infection, which rapidly became septicemia, a generalized infection of the blood. This being well before the arrival of antibiotics, the treatment was management of the resulting high fever (by being wrapped into ice-cold towels) and pain killers. This lasted several weeks; I have, of course, no specific*

memory of the experience of pain, but my sister Csupi told me of the family standing helplessly by my bed for hours on end while I was whinnying like a hurt dog.

Some time around my fifth year I once again came down with infections in both ears, septicemia, but in a much more severe form; I had to have both ears operated on, suffered terribly, and became essentially paralyzed in both legs. After returning from weeks in the hospital, I recall crawling on my belly, then knees on the carpets in our home, and painfully learning to walk all over again—always under the firm and loving hand of Csurka and her mother, Helen. Somehow this passed, apparently without permanent damage (except, of course, to the psyches of each of us in some ways, for how could it not leave some scars?) and our lives went on.

"Yes, well the hospital phoned us to come down and say goodbye to him," said Csupi. "They thought he was going to die."

I hadn't realized how close his life had come to ending before it'd even begun. In my father's telling, the apartment at #2 Szász Károly was a refuge. He lacked for nothing: His Grandma Helen and Uncle Kalman lived in the adjoining building, his best friend Tamas upstairs. On school holidays they'd travel to Szerencs, where Csurka's brother Miklós was the engineer of the massive sugar works there. Once Miklós took him out to survey the vast sugar beet fields, riding in the cab of the narrow-gauge locomotive used to haul the crops back to the plant. Miklós even granted my father a few heart-pounding minutes at the great iron throttle lever. "To say I was in heaven," he later wrote, "is a massive understatement."

"So, Csupi, what was happening outside? Did Muki ever talk about the political situation?"

"No, never. Never about Hitler. He didn't want to scare us. I know that he feared for his job. Of course in the '30s, everyone knew about Hitler's strength building. There was no avoiding it."

I thought back to how my father once described Hungary's relationship with Nazi Germany: He'd called it a *csárdás,* an intricate and clever folk dance. But in the last months, I'd realized the relationship was more complicated and also simpler. Hungary may have been a sharp dancer, but its agenda was crystal-clear. As Europe's nations squared off for the coming bout, Hungary drifted ever closer into Hitler's orbit, lured by an irresistible bit of catnip: The hope of reversing The Treaty of Trianon.

Trianon was Hungary's version of Versailles, the document that ended the First World War for Germany. But Trianon was far harsher: There were no deliberations, no counteroffers, no negotiations. With the stroke of a pen, the treaty gave two thirds of Hungary's territory and two fifths of its people to its neighbors, Romania and Slovakia. It was both a shocking blow and a tailor-made propaganda opportunity, placing in Admiral Horthy's gloved hand a whip with which to unify the nation. Now, with Germany's star ascendant, Hitler hinted that siding with him was Hungary's only chance to reclaim its stolen land.

I thought back to my father's sentimental recollections of the '30s. How he'd never really told me what happened to Helen and Kalman, Tamás and Miklós and all the others. I realized, with a slight shudder, what none of my family then knew: That there was no longer any escaping what was to come. Then my aunt's voice snapped me back. "Hallo? Seth?"

"Sorry, Csupi. I lost myself for a moment there."

Sensing a note of tiredness in my aunt's voice, I rushed to my next question, hoping I sounded more neutral than I felt. "So, Csupi," I said, "what about Jewishness? Was the family observant?"

"Never. We never went to Jewish church. We went to the one on Margit Boulevard, St. Stephen's."

Jewish church?

"So wait, the family went to a *Catholic* church?"

"Yes, Muki and Csurka started going when they moved there, before I was born." Her tone suggested there was nothing out of the ordinary about this. Still, it stuck in my craw, the same way their leaving the Jewish part of town did. As if their faces alone wouldn't give them away. But before I could wedge in another pry bar, Csupi briskly shut the door.

"So tell me, Seth: What do you do for work?"

I sighed quietly, knowing I had no choice but to try again next time. All the same, as we said our goodbyes I sensed a screw turning, drawing me back in time. Over the coming months my conversations with Csupi would become a sort of oracular ritual, a spelunking expedition into caves of ancestral memory. As I followed my family's story into the anxious 1930s, their coming crucible suddenly felt very close, as if only snatched from the previous night's dream. My aunt's recollections, fragile and elliptical though they were, were handholds to which I could cling as I descended into my family's fast-fading memories, and also my own.

29

Portland, December 2017: Winter in Portland is a grey smear, with days-long rains broken by bursts of piercing blue sky. Late that December a freak snowstorm hit, clogging roads and closing schools. Evelyn was nearly eleven, just rounding the cusp when little-kid activities no longer appealed to her. Still, the morning of the snowstorm I snuck out to the garage and cobbled together a crude sled from scrap metal and wood. It was a bit comical—I'm not much of a carpenter—but I don't think I'll ever forget Evelyn's reaction when I presented it to her.

"Wait! What?" she cried, her eyes widening. "You…made this?" Then we both collapsed in laughter. "Uh…thank you!" We trudged to a nearby park, where the sled proved predictably slow and nearly unsteerable. But as we walked home, fingers and toes tingling with cold, I felt a warm glow. My own father had never so much as thrown a ball with me; I knew that in some small way I was rewriting my family story.

In the coming days the snow melted and school reopened. With no work coming in, I turned back to tracing my family's story. Since that first conversation with Aunt Csupi, I'd been fixated on #2 Szász Károly Street. I longed to see the building in my father's time, so I did the next best thing: I googled the address and cross-referenced it with vintage photos of the neighborhood. This led me to a Hungarian website called "Fortepan," an impressive photo archive dating to the earliest days of photography. As I entered the names of the theaters, cafés, and parks that had surfaced in my conversations with Csupi, the Budapest of my father's childhood sprang to life. Then entirely by chance—if I still believed in such a thing—I stumbled onto a photo of the movie theater where my father first watched *The Wizard of Oz.*

The film was a huge deal in Hungary, and the theater—The Corvin, still in business today—was decked out in a custom marquee for the occasion. Even in his final years, *The Wizard of Oz* stirred a childlike wonder in my father. It's not hard to see why: *Magic is real,* it promises. *One escapes—if only temporarily—through transformation.* I studied the photo closely. A boy in the Tintin-style trousers known as "plus fours" stands in front of the theater. For all I knew, my father is just outside the frame, watching the photographer take the shot. But it wasn't Dorothy and the others who occupied my thoughts. It was what was happening outside, and why the darkened theater felt like such a refuge.

By 1938, the sense of an approaching wave was palpable; which way would it break? Soon Hungary's Jews got an answer. That spring, the National Assembly passed the first in a series of laws barring them from public life. Now Jews couldn't practice law or medicine, work as journalists, merchants, or schoolteachers. Over the next three years, further decrees forced Jews to transfer ownership of their businesses to non-Jews, forbid them from marrying—or even consorting with—Gentiles. Jewishness received a new legal definition: Now it was a racial rather than a cultural attribute. It was a subtle distinction, but one that made possible, even palatable, everything to come. *Don't you see?* Hungarians could say. *We're only following the law!*

It was my father's cousin—also named György, or George— who pointed towards the future. A career naval officer before Trianon erased Austro-Hungary's meager coastline, György joined the River Guard, an elite force tasked with patrolling the country's inland waterways. But after the new laws excluded him from military service, he no longer saw a place for himself in the new Hungary. He put his Frommer service pistol to his head. The River Guard provided him with a showy military funeral with a full band and all the honors accorded by his years of faithful service.

To the west, an ascendant Germany flexed its muscles. As Hitler seized Austria and then the Czechoslovakian *Sudetenland,* the English and the French dithered and wrung their hands. No one appeared willing to stand up to the brazen *Führer,* and Hungary saw only opportunity. Bit by bit, nibble by nibble, the country acclimated itself to eating from Hitler's outstretched hand. After years of surreptitious advances and coy glances across the dinner table, now Hungary, garish makeup and all, stepped forward into the light, arm in arm with Hitler's Germany. There would be no turning back.

Virulent seeds began to sprout. The *Nyilaskeresztes Párt*—the Arrow Cross party, Hungary's homegrown fascists—flexed newfound muscle. Their brain trust was a grey and uninspired thinker named Ferenc Szálasi, whose belief in the Magyar race was as mystical as it was political. He drew blue-collar workers, military personnel, and disaffected nationalists by touting the inevitability of "Hungarism," a self-generated ideology he believed would govern a new Europe, one day even the world.

Because Szálasi supported radical land reforms, Admiral Horthy and his aristocratic backers wanted him silenced. In May of 1939, after the Arrow Cross won a surprising 15% of the vote, Horthy banned the party and had Szálasi arrested. For now, the party would bubble just below the surface, but it wasn't the last Hungary would hear from them.

In 1938, sensing the pincers closing on them, my family at last made a move. Up to now, their churchgoing was quiet and unshowy. Now they publicly renounced Judaism and converted to Catholicism. But the Virgin Mary offered them no refuge; as if anticipating their every step, the laws changed once again. Now those with Jewish grandparents—and those who'd converted after 1919—were still Jews, regardless of their religiosity.

Time sped up and slowed down now, a warping that would never truly resolve. Things were moving terrifyingly fast, and yet the Lorinczis were pinned like flies on tarpaper. Should they run? *Could* they run? Incredibly, now such an opportunity presented itself:

> *I can recall only a single occasion when my parents*
> *seriously considered leaving Hungary. An old friend*
> *of my dad's, who had settled in Paris, came for a visit*
> *with his pretty French girlfriend (of mild interest), and*
> *a smashing new green Renault (of immense interest),*

> *and literally begged my parents to come to Paris and accept a position in his bank. My dad's best foreign language was French, he loved all things French, and I believe he was sorely tempted. In the end we of course did not go, I suspect because of the "normalcy" of life in Hungary and the gravitational pull of family and career. The irony of the story lies in the fact that after the war we learned that the friend did not survive, while the four of us did.*

I looked up from my father's memoirs. Reading his words always had a sightly dissociative effect on me, as though he hovered somewhere just beyond my field of vision. I paused to do the math. In 1938 my father was nine years old, the same age I was in 1980. I remembered the election that year, and watching news coverage of the Reagan campaign over my father's shoulder. I don't remember him saying a single word, but as the camera panned across the sea of corn-fed faces I felt a sickening sense of dread, the sense that things were about to go horribly wrong. I wondered how much my father had known in 1938, and how much of it he'd kept to himself.

30

Portland, December 2017: At the sound of the quiet knock, Julianna and I turned to each other with giddy smiles. I opened the door and in swept Renee: Part counselor, part psychonaut, part witch. I hadn't been aware therapists made house calls before now, but then again Renee's no ordinary therapist. We exchanged earnest hugs and chatted over a pot of tea, and then Julianna led us upstairs.

Evelyn was at her grandmother's; we had all the time in the world. As Julianna and I prepared our nests of blankets, Renee sat her bag down on the credenza and busied herself with vials and a tiny digital scale. "So, this is toad," she said, proffering a tiny baggie filled with glittering crystals.

As Renee measured out the medicine I plastered on what I hoped was a confident-looking smile. My pulse was racing; was that sweat I felt on my brow? Julianna squeezed my hand. A few minutes later, Renee turned to us and offered me a wooden pipe and a lighter. Pressing myself upright against the bed, I spared a nervous glance into the bowl, where a pinch of crystals sat on a bed of dried herbs. "The herbs don't do anything; they're just there to give the medicine some body," explained Renee. One last look at Julianna and her reassuring smile. Then I exhaled slowly, raised the pipe to my lips, and touched flame to bowl.

It's the sensory details that linger with me now: a taste like acrid plastic, the aroma of burning cellophane. As I felt the growing *whoosh* in my eardrums, I set down the pipe with as much care as I could muster and leaned back. On its face it was patently ridiculous, the idea I might find salvation by inhaling amphibian poison. And yet here I was. Or, I should say, I wasn't. As my back found the bed's embrace I felt myself falling into darkness. A final, perplexing image: A great chrysanthemum unfolding inside my skull. Then I was gone.

I'd first heard about toad a few weeks before, when I met with Renee to unpack my recent ayahuasca experiences. She cracked a knowing smile as I described the medicine's characteristic imagery—those endless, proto-digital patterns—and the sense that I was venturing deep into uncharted territory. "I don't even know what's mine anymore," I said. "There's all my personal stuff—like, what am I doing with my life?—but behind it there's this backbeat of anxiety. It's like a familial source code. I think about the times they lived through, how dark they were. And there's this place I keep imagining, this villa my father told me about when I was young."

"Tell me more."

"At the end of the war, when things got really bad, my family hid out in this villa. I really don't know anything about it, except that it was somewhere in the Buda Hills. But I keep imagining it in ayahuasca. Like, I can almost see it, and it's like I have business there." I paused for a moment. "It's like there's some death-fantasy that has to play out."

"Is getting close to death a problem?" asked Renee. "Dying and hiding are such rich metaphors; I wonder if there's information for you there. Maybe some part of you needs to go there to die, to set the present version of yourself free."

I sat silent for a moment. "I get that. But even in ayahuasca, there's a part that still doesn't want to let go, that's still clinging to the side of the pool."

"Maybe you should try toad."

"Um...what?"

"Toad is a medicine that's collected from the Sonoran desert toad, hence the name. The active molecule is known as 5-MeO-DMT; it's a toxin, technically, but it's also a visionary substance. And while I believe all medicines take you to the same place—to unity, to the state of dissolution—some people describe toad as the apex. The template for all the others."

"Huh. Okay. Sounds a little frightening, but...I want to try it."

Now, in my bedroom, I wondered just what it was I'd said yes to. As the flower unfolded inside me I felt myself leaving *here* and going *there*, to a place that defies description. All I can summon back now is utter and enveloping darkness, the sense that I was leaving everything I'd ever known behind.

Imagine yourself quarry jumping at night, stepping off a cliff into total darkness. Now imagine the instant before you hit the water stretching into a second, two seconds, five seconds, ten. In those first moments of toad that's how I felt, and it was utterly terrifying. I fell into a void: nothing to see, nothing to hear, nothing to taste or touch or smell. A crushing wave of fear pressed in on me. *Was this dying?* Then it relented and it was just me and the void.

Ayahuasca suggests there are infinite dimensions beyond the ones we ordinarily sense. In toad, those realms were compressed into one, or perhaps none. There were no mirrors to tell me who I was, nothing to confirm the identity I'd spent my whole life constructing. I didn't even have thoughts, if that's possible. It took a moment to acclimate to the silence, but once I did I realized something that changed everything. The Voice, my internal critic, was gone.

Even in MDMA, even in ayahuasca, the Voice might be quiet for long stretches, but it was always there. This was different. Freed from my caustic inner monologue, I saw the truth. *I existed; it did not.* Something shifted, the *pop* of some internal soap bubble. The Voice was nothing but a string of ones and zeros. It was a code, and that meant it could be rewritten.

Then it was over. As I opened my eyes and the familiar landmarks of this world winked back into being, I saw Renee and Julianna studying me with curious expressions. I'd only been gone a few minutes, but I wasn't the same person who'd left. As if from very far away, I heard my own voice speaking. "I know this sounds crazy," it said, "but I feel like I've been given my life back."

I don't care if it was trippy or trite: It was true.

It'd take some time for me to see it, but those jarring minutes I spent in toad were a capstone, the final leg in the journey that'd led me from the revelations of MDMA to that cautious email from my childhood neighbor to ayahuasca. Even those childhood earaches, when I felt abandoned to a pitiless universe; all of them were asking me to see with fresh eyes, to let go of the stories that'd kept me safe and small. I knew I couldn't change my past or rewrite my family's ancestral memories. It was probably too late to change my personality. But it was truly my life I was living now, and it was up to me what I should do with it.

31

Portland, January 2018: As the calendar ticked over into 2018, I sensed a quickening. I wasn't sure how the book I'd started writing was going to take shape, or if I even had the skill to pull it off in the first place. But as I traced my family's story, concrete images began to form, details of a long-forgotten photograph finally emerging from the developer bath. I was on the hunt, and I felt infused with a welcome sense of purpose.

> *Now, where was I? 1938, the last moment before the storm clouds closed over our lives in a darkness which, in a sense, has never entirely lifted since then. I have a vivid and marvelously pleasant recollection of our last peacetime vacation; a trip the four of us made by train and ship to the (then) Italian fishing port on the Adriatic called Portorose.*
>
> *Our vacation home was a "pensione" high above the beautiful little fishing port, amid palm trees, cacti, and other wonders I had only read about in books and dreamt of one day seeing; everything was perfect. The sea was a deep blue, the hills lush with flowers, the ships in the harbor little toys for my amusement and the food delicious. Every day opened to new wonders, the greatest of which was the arrival of a sleek Italian destroyer whose name I still remember: "Generale Papa."*
>
> *It seems that I was not alone in my admiration. Csupi, then fourteen and becoming keenly aware of the possibilities offered by the opposite sex, managed to attract*

the attention of a slim, handsome midshipman aged perhaps eighteen, who shyly asked her for a walk. Our dad, who witnessed the scene, then descended on the hapless young man in Olympian wrath, sent him on his way, and delivered a tremendous slap—or was it a spanking on the behind?—to my poor and humiliated sister. Nor was this all; we heard on the BBC sometime in 1943 or so that the Generale Papa was attacked by British warplanes in the Mediterranean and blown up. That showed them how risky it was to make untoward advances towards Csupi Lorinczi!

I looked up from the page, a lump forming in my throat. Here, at last, my father had touched on the darkness gathering on the horizon. I'd knew he'd acknowledge it sooner or later; what I didn't expect was that I'd be able see it with my own two eyes.

A few days later, I saw a padded envelope protruding from our mailbox. The return address was in Laramie, Wyoming. After a moment of puzzlement it came to me: A few weeks before, Deborah had told me she was getting the family's 8mm home movies transferred to DVDs. I brought the envelope inside, and that's when I felt the hand on my chest.

It wasn't a real hand, of course. But I don't know how else to describe it: A sensation of ghostly fingers pushing down on my sternum. It spooked me; I couldn't tell if it was beckoning me forward or holding me back. And so I set the envelope aside and didn't think about it for a week or so. Finally, one quiet afternoon, I took my laptop and the DVDs to a quiet room and shut the door.

When I finally got the balky disc reader in my laptop to work, I was confused. The screen looked like a snarl of static, and it was a moment before I realized I was watching an ancient black-and-white film strip. The static resolved into a long, jerky sweep tracing a panorama of mountains, then a fuzzy exterior shot of a grandiose hotel and spa straight out of a Wes Anderson film. A split second later I finally understood what I was seeing: Here, etched onto whickering frames of film, was footage of my family's final vacation in Portorose, the one I'd just been reading about.

I stared, agog. I'd seen it once before, but that was decades ago; I must have been seven or eight. Our library of home movies was mostly footage of my mother, and after she was gone my father just didn't seem to want to drag the projector out of the closet anymore.

How had the film even made it here? I knew of literally two other objects—an oil portrait of Csurka's Uncle Desző and a scrap of upholstery she'd knitted—that even made it out of Hungary. My family had left everything behind, and yet this single reel had somehow survived. Now, as the film unspooled itself, something inside me came undone, and I looked into a universe I'd never dreamt I might see.

Onscreen, Aunt Csupi and my nine-year-old father rough-house on the hotel's manicured lawn. It's the revelation of movement that takes my breath away, of time not frozen as in photographs but liquid, supple, alive. The film cuts movement into frames, sixteen to the second, and occasionally the eye—*the brain*—fails to smooth them into continuity. But my father's slightly rolling gait, beamed through the decades, is perfectly legible. For the very first time I see him as the rest of the world must have: A soft and slightly overfed Jewish boy.

I feel as though I'm deep in ayahuasca again. I'm flooded by a nearly painful feeling of empathy, and it seems obvious my family's story is preordained, that everything that will be has already been written. A thought of my mother arises: She is only a year old when this film is being made, but even now she's wending towards her inevitable union with my father, and thus with me.

And I understand for the first time how uncomfortable my own childhood struggles must have made my father: I must have reminded him of the powerless little boy he'd once been. After my mother died, and when things with Irene got so awful, he could've taken time to bond with me. Instead, he'd more or less disappeared. I'd do literally anything to protect Evelyn from sadness or harm; why hadn't my father done the same for me?

Just like that, the film ended. The final shot is up a rough dirt lane, stone cottages dwarfed by fog-wreathed hills. There's no focal point, as good a metaphor as any for what's about to unfold. I turned off the laptop. The electric feeling inside me was beginning to fade, though I still felt altered. I opened up the filing cabinet, pulled out my father's memoirs, and flipped to the page about Portorose. Now my own emotions gave his words a new edge. It was getting very close to the end.

> *I have the keenest, almost palpable memory of our departure after a heavenly four weeks at Portorose; the last thing I did was to wander, alone, through that sumptuous garden, and say goodbye, aloud, to every palm tree, bush, and bench I had so loved. The pain of losing so much carefree happiness still constricts my throat more than a half-century later.*

32

Laramie, January 2018: I stepped outside the shelter of Laramie's austere airport and into the frigid winter air. And there she was: My cousin Deborah, waiting for me at the curb. Not much had changed: The halo of hair floating above her parka had gone grey but her eyes still sparkled with kindness.

"Settino!" she cried, and my heart gave a little leap. That was the nickname my father had given me after a trip to Italy, where pronouncing the "th" in "Seth" proved challenging to the locals.

I was glad I'd come.

"So, this is the co-op, and over there's the library…." As we rolled through snow-hushed streets, Deborah gave me a guided tour. "I'm about twenty minutes out of town but…Oh! That place has really good donuts but they're closed. Dammit!"

I thought back to the years after my father had died, when phone calls with Deborah would leave me feeling physically cramped. And as easy as saying *yes* to this trip had felt, in the last weeks I'd felt an old anxiety. Maybe Deborah's volatility would fire back up, releasing a flood of buried grievances. Behind this was the fear that the medicine work hadn't really changed me after all. That I'd still feel the need to hold my cousin at arm's length, or judge her essential neediness.

But Deborah seemed gentler now, more settled. I saw a woman facing the radically altered landscape of her life through clear eyes. I felt myself relaxing as we drove on and the subdivisions became sparser, ceding to cattle pasture and grassland. Eventually we stopped before a modern ranch house. "This is it!" Deborah said. She paused, a wistful note entering her voice. "Isai and I only moved in last fall. I don't even know if I'm going to stay."

In the kitchen, I began dicing carrots and onions for a wintry stew while Deborah uncorked a bottle of wine. Outside, the hills hunched in their stony silence. As she unpacked the story of her two decades with Isai his ghost felt like a tangible presence, and I wasn't sure it was a benevolent one. His life had been so much more challenging than mine. A few months after his birth, the Nazis invaded Ukraine. After his father was killed in combat, Isai's mother literally hid him in dugouts and cellars from death squads.

Isai was blunt and plain-spoken, and I thought I'd read him like an open book. Now I saw that in my haste, I'd skipped entire chapters. Behind his twinkling smile lay a darker side: A man suspicious of his own family, who questioned his wife's loyalty. "Oh, it got really bad a couple of years ago," Deborah told me. "I actually kicked him out for a while. He got so angry and paranoid, like he didn't trust anyone anymore."

"It makes me wonder how my father was when he arrived here," I said, savoring a bite of venison. "I mean, it's hard to imagine parents as young people. Was he always…you know, himself?"

"I actually tried to look up your dad's immigration papers once. I never found them, but I did find this." She got up and went to her bedroom, returning with a tiny black-and-white photograph of my father. He looks about eighteen, uncharacteristically gangly in high-waisted trousers and a wide-lapeled shirt, standing before a stately low-slung building. Surrounding it, improbably, are palm trees. I studied the photo intensely.

"Where the hell is this?" I asked. "I've never seen it before. I mean, for starters, where was it taken?"

"It must be from Europe, before he came here, but I have no idea where or when."

"There are all these periods about which I know *nothing*. I mean, he barely talked about the time you were growing up. What was it like?"

"Well…it was just so *anxious*. There were always Hungarians coming through to stay with us. You know, like refugees. Everyone just seemed so traumatized by the war."

"Was he?"

"He was unreliable, like an alcoholic. He couldn't be trusted to show up for anything. Of course, life at home kind of sucked for him. His wife Ruth's parents lived in the basement. They looked down on him, like he wasn't good enough for their daughter. One morning he was standing in front of the fridge with the door open. Just, like, reveling in the sight of a pitcher of orange juice and a carton of eggs, you know? And then Ruth's mom came out from their basement apartment. She walked right over to the refrigerator and shut the door in his face. And she said: 'Beggars can't be choosers.'"

"Brutal. After he died, my Aunt Sheila said he was the most self-assured and confident man she'd ever met. I mean, I didn't feel the same way but still: I'm kind of floored."

We were silent for a moment. Now another of those memories bubbled up inside me. "Okay, here's something," I said. "I nearly forgot this, but when I was still pretty young, he told me that in his first years in America, he was really scared of using public bathrooms."

"Yes! He was terrified of people seeing he was Jewish. And of large crowds, like at fairgrounds and concerts. He avoided them like the plague. And did you know that when I was young, he moved us from a Jewish neighborhood to a Protestant one?"

"Fascinating! Like how Muki moved the family from Buda to Pest. Speaking of which, when he took me to Budapest to say goodbye to Antal and Pal, we went to his middle school. In fact, he wrote about it. Hang on." I went to fetch my laptop and read aloud:

> *In the first grade of every school we were confronted, in every classroom, with a map of post-Trianon Hungary surrounded by a bloody crown of thorns and surmounted by the legend "No, No, Never!"—a mocking refrain of the very name of Trianon. I cannot begin to tell you how all-pervasive this motif was in all of our school experiences, and what degree of fanaticism this created, as it was meant to.*

> *Much, much worse was to come. Over the next years, the occasional snide, semi-concealed antisemitic remarks or behavior of my classmates gradually became bolder and more violent, as Hungary drifted closer into the German orbit and people somehow sensed that the*

*inhibitions against this sort of conduct slowly, imper-
ceptibly became more and more relaxed, except in the
classrooms of a few exceptionally dedicated and upright teachers. The process was so gradual and subtle at
first that one could not even be sure of its nature—and
denial itself became a line of defense; the "accidental"
shove or kick during gymnastics class or a game, the
ambiguous flaunting of Christian symbols gradually
gave way to more and more overt—and more and more
tolerated—acts of hostility and aggression. I tried to
conceal all of this from my parents so as to spare them
the pain, and hide my own.*

"I bet that was so awful for him," Deborah said. "Did you know that every day his classmates would shove him down on the playground? Sometimes they'd pin him down and pull down his pants to check if he was 'still Jewish.'"

"Jesus Christ. He never told me that." Suddenly my father's rigid avoidance around the topic of sex made so much more sense.

"Yeah, there were like all these suppressed memories. When he'd come home from work, he'd talk to me before he talked to Ruth. And sometimes he'd tell me about what'd happened, back in Hungary. I mean, I was only like ten years old. He'd get this kind of panicked look, and it was like he just had to tell someone. It seemed like he couldn't control it; it was like an orgasm."

My stomach gave a tiny lurch. Much as I wanted this moment to pass, to push it back down into the slimy recess from which it had come, now another memory came back to me. A year before he died, my father and I took a brief road trip. Like that random conversation about Korea with Ruth, I don't know what prompted me to ask about the period after he left his first American family, before he met my mother. But an uncharacteristic brittleness came over him. After a tense moment of silence, he told me that after he left Ruth, he and Deborah shared an apartment for a time. "We lived more as man and wife," he said. "Of course, there was nothing inappropriate," he quickly added. "She really kept house for me."

I never forgot what slipped past my father's lawyerly circumspection that day. I didn't for an instant believe there was anything inappropriate about their relationship, if one means a sexual transgression. But now, feeling the jagged puzzle pieces in my hand, I understood how little I'd really known about my father. And his ambivalence around Deborah, the woman he'd raised like his own daughter.

Deborah seemed strangely content, like what she'd told me was no big deal. She'd been forced to be an adult long before she should have; after a moment, I realized I had too.

"Okay," I said. "This is a lot to take in." We sat in silence for a moment, and I realized how tired I actually was. I glanced at the clock. "Love, I have to hit it. Thanks so much for welcoming me here. I'm going to give Julianna one last call." We embraced and I walked back outside.

33

Laramie, January 2018: Outside, the sky was an icy smattering of stars. I pulled up Julianna's number and hoped she'd pick up.

"Baby!" she cooed. "I'm so glad you're there. How's it going?"

"It's good! It sounds kind of grandiose, but I think this is what all the work of the last years has been for. The dismantling of myself. I feel really different around Deborah now, like I don't need to protect myself from her mood swings. And I'm learning so much. You wouldn't believe it! As hard as parts of my childhood were, I think Deborah got the worst of it. Growing up in my father's first household sounded like a nightmare."

"Well, it's a really big deal your being there. And I know it must mean a lot to Deborah. Is she okay?"

"I…think so? But I see now that she doesn't really *do* anything, not in a productive-member-of-society way. I mean, she's got a framed note from Elie Weisel on her wall, from some graduate course she took with him. And a study group with Saul Bellow. But she never actually did anything with it. She worked at an insurance corporation for a few years, and then when Isai showed up she just kind of dropped out."

"You didn't come from an easy family. Maybe it's enough to just be her witness."

"Yeah. I definitely couldn't have done this a year ago."

"I know. Keep going."

We said our goodnights and hung up. But as I stepped back inside and readied myself for bed, I felt a growing unease. Deborah had put me in Isai's room; it was his bed I was climbing into, the one in which he'd shot himself. New mattress, the hole in the ceiling patched and painted. But no amount of scrubbing could dispel my dread. The ghost I'd felt circling me before suddenly felt terrifyingly close, and I realized it wasn't Isai's spirit haunting me. It was the specter of my own failure. I was nearing fifty and I hadn't done anything with my life. Surely it was too late now. Now the ghost shape-shifted: It was the Voice, the internal critic I thought I'd finally put to rest. *This was your only chance,* it whispered soundlessly.

A cold wave of despair washed over me. I lay there in the dark, wondering in earnest if this was what a demonic possession felt like. It felt as though some spirit had entered my body to take control of it, using me towards its own ends. Would I resist it? *Could* I resist it? My annihilation felt terrifyingly close, the panting of a large animal in a dark forest. There was so little to stop me from simply stepping off the train right here and now, just like Isai had. Surely that was better than carrying this feeling of failure even one hour longer. *It would be so easy.* My own daughter had seen it, and yet I could barely name it myself.

I'd wrestled with demons before. In medicine, in my thousand sleepless nights with Julianna. I saw now how I'd always judged Deborah for her neediness. Her passivity and her inability to make something of herself were aspects of myself I'd desperately tried to deny. Now, lying in this literal death-bed, I couldn't outrun the truth: That if I couldn't accept her in all her human messiness, I had no hope of accepting myself, either. All the gifts of the medicine work, the deepening bond with Julianna and Evelyn, none of it was any good if I couldn't share it with everyone, my complicated cousin included.

Here was the nub, the truth I hadn't dared face: I *had* allowed most of my life to slip by. I'd squandered nearly everything I'd been given, and now I'd run out of time. We all had. The Earth had decided for us, throwing in the towel, telling us it'd had enough. Somewhere, very far away, 150 acres of rain forest was vanishing each minute. Earth's lungs were collapsing, species after species winking out with less fanfare than a sparkler on the Fourth of July. There was no longer any time to wait.

Now I thought of how far I'd come, how the stories I'd thought were me had broken apart and blown away. I'd faced the darkest truths of my life, and I'd survived. I was willing to keep going, or at least I was willing to be willing. And with this I felt my dread subside and another door open.

Earlier that night when the conversation had turned to Hungary, I felt something stirring. As Deborah rattled off the names of our family and friends there I felt a quiet thrill. "Antal looks just like your father," she said. "It's seriously freaky!" Still, I believed I could uncover my family's story without feeling the weight of Budapest's air on my skin or hearing the quiet slosh of the Danube. But when Deborah mentioned the Labor Service—Hungary's wartime conscription service for Jews and other "enemies of the state"—a corner piece of the jigsaw slipped into place. "You know, Poki's dad wrote a memoir about it," she offered. "You should ask him!"

Now I was catapulted back to my visit to Budapest, twenty years earlier. It was a punishing trip, my terminally ill father's farewell tour. One morning as we traversed the city in a hired car, he directed the driver to a nondescript alley in Inner Pest. My father and I got out, and for a long moment we stood looking through the archway. He cleared his throat quietly. "This," he finally said, "is where I came to register for the Labor Service."

That was the summer of 1944, the year everything finally came apart. Now, lying in Isai's bed, the ghosts of despair circling me, I felt myself clicking into my family's story—and my own—in a way I hadn't allowed before. I understood that returning to Hungary was no longer optional. I needed to find my father there, so that I could finally put him to rest.

This was your only chance, the Voice whispered again. *Fuck you,* I whispered back.

34

Portland, March 2018: When a caterpillar enters its cocoon for its momentous second act, it dissolves itself. It disintegrates into goo, then reformulates with a completely new set of body parts. The blueprints for these new organs are contained in clusters of cells that guide and direct the new construction. Best of all, some scientist-poet thought to give them an evocative name: Imaginal discs.

Over the weeks that followed my trip to Laramie, I clung to the metaphor of the imaginal disc. I felt like I was disintegrating, and as I did the stories of who I'd been fell away, sometimes painfully and sometimes with little more than a grateful sigh. As Julianna and I pressed ever closer to one other, the foxholes I'd fought so bitterly to defend melted back into the ground. I no longer bristled in indignation when she asked me to help out in the garden or perform needed home repairs. We were healing ourselves, and I felt the dawning power of collaboration. New growth appeared, the long-dormant earth bursting with fresh life. Music, dancing, and sex cautiously reappeared.

We'd sat roughly a dozen ayahuasca ceremonies each by now, often together but sometimes on our own. Each was profound and profoundly different, though there were through lines. I threw up here; I threw up there. Once, I thought I was having a heart attack. But through them all, a signal was becoming clearer: It told me that my work was not in these dark basements but outside, in the real world. It was time to do something with what I'd been shown.

Writing this book no longer felt like a crazy indulgence, but a quest drawing me towards my essential truth. Julianna's strength was returning, her gut healing as the autoimmune disorder gradually faded. With it came a flush of art, the likes of which I'd never seen: intricate botanical paintings, depictions of unearthly shrines and symbols. Something in her was blossoming, and it was inspiring me to dig ever deeper into my own inner sanctums.

Those ayahuasca ceremonies provided their own backbeat, an alternate calendar to orient ourselves to. If they tended to be solemn affairs, at times nearly sepulchral in their silence, laughter and play had their places too. One night, deep in the medicine, I trailed behind Julianna as she literally crawled to the altar for a second pour. When the wizened facilitator asked me how much I wanted, I nodded towards my shuddering wife with a bright smile: "I'll have what the little lady's having!"

I was learning how to dance.

I mean that literally. At the end of ceremony, the final half hour is often reserved for a stupendous dance party. You will never dance as joyously as you do after eight hours spent weeping and throwing up into a plastic bucket. These spontaneous celebrations also served to illuminate Julianna's preternatural beauty. Watching her move, I was sure I could never want anyone as badly. I was returning to my life, the one I'd been ripped away from decades before. And it was happening in real time, right before my eyes.

I wasn't the only one entranced by imaginal discs. As this book was taking shape, songs began coming to Julianna. They were totally unlike the music she and I had made together. I'd been obsessed with recreating the sounds of the '60s, and Julianna—sometimes gamely, sometimes less so—had followed suit. But the music she was writing now didn't seem to reference anything either of us had ever heard before. It felt nakedly devotional, an epic poem tracing her creative descent. Some pieces were simple drones; others built on massed percussion and thick layers of vocals. None of them specifically referenced ayahuasca, but it was clear that the medicine was opening something wondrous and deep in her. I was watching someone I thought I'd known well morph right before my eyes. And if I felt a slight—okay, sometimes not-so-slight—sting at the knowledge that Julianna no longer needed me to make music, it was impossible to deny what she was bringing forth. These were songs about plumbing the depths to find herself, and their simple beauty often reduced me to tears.

Me? I was ready to let go of music. One morning, I descended the stairs to my basement studio, took my usual place before the mixing console, and looked around. All around me, hundreds of tiny lightbulbs pierced the darkness. I'd always loved the sense of envelopment here, like I was at the controls of a spaceship. But magnificent though it was, I knew this ship wasn't going anywhere. It was time to try something new.

Julianna and I had been talking about selling our house for months. Actually, she'd been doing the talking; I'd been doing the avoiding. Every time she brought it up, I felt my blood pressure rise. Why should we leave? Our home was beautiful, and the Portland housing market was so superheated we'd never afford one as nice.

What I hadn't allowed myself to acknowledge, aside from Julianna's impatience, was how afraid I felt. Afraid of giving up the hollow safety of our home, the studio where I no longer made music. Afraid to acknowledge that neither of us earned enough, and that I didn't want my face pushed in it by being denied a loan. Some part of me knew this place was a dead end, but still I couldn't let go. The part of me that had awakened in ayahuasca was in struggle with the part that wanted to stay asleep.

I heard soft footfalls on the stairs behind me. "Hi babe," said Julianna. "Mind if I join you?" I nodded my assent and she sat down next to me.

"This place is so beautiful," she said after a moment. "You really created something special here."

"Thanks. It really *is* me, in a way. I mean, all the weird stray-dog pieces of gear, the handmade-ness of it." I paused for a moment, unsure of how to proceed. "But it took so much work. I don't know how to just let it all go. It'd feel like such a waste."

"You didn't waste anything. You did what you knew how to do, and you created a temple down here. But here's the thing: You feel like you can't let go of all this," she said, sweeping her hand across the starscape of twinkling lights. "But you have *no idea* what will come to take its place once you make room for it."

I glanced around the studio at the piles of gear, the tape decks and cables, microphones and stands, speakers and guitars and vacuum tubes. A quiet voice sounded inside: *Let it go.*

I turned to face Julianna. "Okay. I'm ready."

And so we began to plan our next move: What kind of house we'd look for and where, how we'd afford it. It was time to decommission the studio, and so I began to sell off all the gear

I'd accumulated. One morning, as I struggled to dismantle the soundproofing baffles, I looked around in vain for my socket wrenches.

"Hey where's the tools that were at the top of the stairs?" I called up to the kitchen. Half-hearing Julianna's muffled reply coming from the kitchen, I cursed quietly and stomped upstairs. She was in the kitchen, wrapping plates in layers of newspaper. "Hey, my socket wrenches were out here. Where'd they go?"

"Yeah, they've been sitting there for a week and a half. I nearly tripped on them, so I put them away."

"Well I was using them," I said, a harsh edge creeping into my voice. "I wish you wouldn't do stuff like that."

Julianna rolled her eyes and I felt my body tense for the familiar face-off: First she'd complain that I left my things all over the house, then I'd angrily explain why having her derail my projects was so irritating. We'd squabble for a few minutes before breaking to our corners of the house for a few hours. In the past, when it was really bad, the chill would sometimes last for days.

But here's where it got weird. Instead of tensing for a showdown, we passed through some membrane instead. We'd had this same stupid argument hundreds of times before. We'd both memorized our lines down pat, knew our roles. What if we chose a different way? I relaxed my face and dropped my shoulders.

"This is…trippy," I said. "Do you feel it? This is some kind of reenactment. We were just about to have this fight all over again, and…who even cares? I'm sorry I left my tools out."

"And I'm sorry I put them back without asking you." Julianna's face looked beatific and calm. "This is that place of neutrality I've been talking about. We can have that argument, or we can come closer to one another. Nothing is personal; it's all a dream. And this is what waking up in the dream looks like."

"This is the ayahuasca, isn't it?"

"No. This is us."

35

Portland, April 2018: One rainy Sunday, Julianna, Evelyn, and I drove to see a nondescript ranch house on a cul-de-sac. The paint was a faded skin tone; the lawn was roached from decades of Roundup. It was clear that this wasn't one of Portland's hotter open houses; no warm chocolate-chip cookies or red wine waiting in the breakfast nook. But as Julianna took in the open-plan dining room I saw her lighting up. "I think this is it," she whispered to me. "I think this is where we're supposed to live. We take out these two walls and it's perfect. And imagine the yard planted with natives and fruit trees!"

"I think Mom's right," added Evelyn, swooshing through the pink-and-purple painted bedrooms. "I love this place!"

Um, you do? I thought. Our daughter's tastes ran towards the more modern and polished: In other words, anything but this. I just kept my mouth shut, hoping the enchantment would last.

It did. Somehow, in a hyper-aggressive real estate market, no one else ended up making an offer. It sat for months, just waiting for us. Simultaneously, through the grapevine, we found a family interested in buying our current home. It took some fancy financial footwork, but the deals ended up closing on the very same day. I'd expected tension, stress, maybe even a simmering spat between Julianna and I. But when the giant moving truck arrived, I felt only calm. Everything magically came together that day, from shuttling our one remaining rabbit, Nutcake, to taking the back door off its hinges so the movers could get the piano into the basement. By the time they left it was nearly dark. Feeling slightly shellshocked, we went out to share a quiet dinner. Later, as Julianna and I pulled into the driveway of our new home—Evelyn was at her cousins'—I saw a flash of motion by the car door. It was a small brown rabbit, the first of many I'd see around the house. It seemed like it'd been waiting for us to arrive.

The bones of our new house were good, but we knew we wanted to change things. Without quite knowing what we were doing (did I mention I'm a woeful carpenter?) we began to reshape our home: Tearing down walls, adding a skylight, reviving the long-neglected yard.

It wasn't easy, but things that should have felt disastrous became hilarious instead. Once, as I wriggled up to the attic crawlspace to run new electrical lines, I stepped through sheet rock and fell almost to the concrete floor below. Another time, a misaligned drain sent a waterfall cascading into the basement. In the past, these mishaps would have triggered serious waves of teeth-gnashing, even self-loathing. Now they were just comedic. Even when it felt like nothing was going right, we could do no wrong. We called it "temple-building," and I knew that it was rewriting our story.

As we remade the house we remade ourselves, too. For nearly half a year the three of us lived in the basement, preparing all our meals with a microwave and a single electric burner. Evelyn wasn't enthusiastic about this arrangement, and at times I wondered if we were on the verge of a full-scale mutiny. But a little hardship turned out to be just the glue we needed. We laughed a lot and grew closer, and I watched as my daughter blossomed from a little kid into a smart, independent, and emotionally wise young person.

Five months later, we emerged from the basement and took stock of our new home. We'd stretched ourselves far beyond what I thought possible, building a sturdy kitchen island, ripping up and leveling the strangely mismatched flooring, replacing and expanding windows and doors to let in more light, more energy, more flow. In the garden, Julianna's native brilliance shone in everything she touched. Under her gentle prodding, the heavily treated lawn transformed into a bountiful wild space.

I couldn't believe how different my life felt from even a couple of years before. Once I put myself forward as a freelancer, my writing portfolio began to fill. Julianna began offering sound-healing sessions to clients, and with very little effort, her practice began to grow and take on a life of its own. It felt like we'd pulled off a daring escape from our old lives, just in the nick of time; all we'd had to do was surrender.

Then, one morning early in 2019, a signal arrived. It was early, still dark outside. Something—the rustling of trees, the unfamiliar creakings of our new house—had awakened me. In the stillness I heard a voice speak inside my head, quiet but unnervingly clear: *Go to Budapest.*

I blinked myself awake. Had I been dreaming? Then it spoke again: *Go now.*

For as long as I could remember, I'd longed for a message so clear there'd be no way to refuse it. Now that it'd finally arrived, I felt unsure. Nothing about it made sense. Not the timing, not the expense, not the distraction from…from what, exactly? Wasn't the point of being a freelancer that I was *free*? The thought tumbled over a few more times before I finally fell back to sleep.

The next day, the quiet tickle in my ear refused to subside. Ever since I'd settled on writing the book, I'd believed I could do it from the comfort of my own home. Now that seemed preposterous. My family's story was somewhere out there, in the streets and alleyways of Budapest. An image swam into view: A stately old house in a forest somewhere, surrounded by evergreens. It was the villa, the one my family had sheltered in at the end of the war. Suddenly it seemed imperative that I find it. And so with a mixture of dread and relief, I looked up airfares to Budapest.

"How long should I go for?" I asked Julianna.

"A month at least!" she said. "You can't hunt ghosts in a week. Stay; go as deep as you can."

"Woof. Okay. Wow. This is happening, isn't it? This is what I've been working towards the whole time and didn't even know it."

"Just think of the food! Things you probably haven't tasted since your grandmother was alive. It's going to be a sour cream bloodbath!"

"Yeah, but that may not necessarily be a good thing."

"It's going to be incredible!"

In the days that followed, my excitement began to build. But behind this was a distinct sense of unease. Viktor Orbán, Hungary's prime minister since 2010, has been described as "a smart Donald Trump." The few remaining independent media outlets describe an increasingly anti-immigrant and antisemitic environment. Incredibly, some people who lived through the Socialist years describe the environment today as being even worse.

Could it really be true? I reached out to my cousin Pal, the one who'd forwarded those beautiful photos of Muki from the First World War. He seemed genuinely excited at the prospect of seeing me, but he had little to say about the political situation. The same with Poki, who's so close he might as well be family: His father was my grandparents' family doctor back in the '40s. But when we reconnected over a video call, he was strangely tight-lipped. What was it they couldn't tell me?

Now I was startled by yet another invitation from out of the blue. It was a text message from my sister Stacey:

Hi! This is crazy, but...can I come to Budapest with you?

36

Portland, April 2019: Uncomplicated as visiting Deborah had felt, my answer to Stacey was equally clear: *No.*

It wasn't that we didn't get along. Just as the ice between Deborah and me had thawed in the last few years, so had it with Stacey. She was my sister, after all. But siblings, they say, have different parents. If I retained only a few fragmented memories of my mother, Stacey—just shy of two when Rhonda died—had none at all. Nor was she interested in looking for them. Whenever I'd try to steer the conversation in that direction, Stacey would dart away like a startled hummingbird.

The few times I shared what I'd been writing with her, it bombed. "Hm, I don't recall Dad being like that," she'd say, meaning: *Your memories are wrong.* Once, she even offered to "edit" an essay I'd written about my own childhood. I politely declined. All this to say: There was no way she was coming to Hungary with me. I was the one who'd reconnected with friends and family there, spent all this time researching our history. It was *my* trip to *my* country, goddamnit, and I wasn't going to let her ruin it with her blitheness and general lack of gravitas.

As it so happened, the weekend after her request I was slated to sit an ayahuasca ceremony, this time without Julianna. As I hauled my bundles up the driveway of the now-familiar complex, I was happy to recognize a few friends among the apprehensive first-timers. Back in the now-familiar basement, I set up my nest and tried to ground. Beside me, a young woman was preparing her own area with crystals and paraphernalia. That's when I saw the talisman.

It was a round wooden token printed with a symbol: A pair of double-ended arrows crossed over one another. I recognized it at once. In early Christianity it was an allusion to the *Ichthys* symbol, the "Jesus fish" stuck on the ass ends of millions of American cars. But in Hungary, it's something very differ-ent: the symbol of the Arrow Cross, Hungary's homegrown Nazis. It's their version of the swastika. But before I could ask the woman about the token, the wizened facilitator began to speak, silencing all other conversation.

Though I opted for a less heroic dose than usual, that night's journey was hardly easeful. As I fell into the place beyond words, I recognized how thoroughly my family's tragedy had ensnared me, working its way into my very DNA. My thoughts turned to Budapest and the journey I was about to undertake. I'd gone and booked myself a month-long trip, and I had next to no idea what I was doing. It seemed both preposterous and wildly wasteful.

A dark stab of fear pressed into my gut. In earlier ayahuas-ca journeys, I'd often imagined myself into the past: Standing on the bank of the Danube in the bitter cold, the muzzle of a Hungarian Army carbine pressed to the base of my neck. But these morbid visions were just play-acting; they had nothing to teach me. Those lives had never been mine to live, those deaths not mine to die. I couldn't change what had happened on the riverbank. But it was up to me whether or not I'd live the rest of my life in its shadow.

As the medicine dragged me into its subterranean realms, I felt a new knowing take hold: that my job was not to reenact this suffering, but to transmute it. The medicine was asking me to face the sadness I was born into, to accept it, even to love it. I'd approached this molten core before, never understanding that it wasn't a destination but a portal into something far wider and greater. That through it lay my life.

I knew something else: That my work in ayahuasca was com-plete, at least for now. It was time for me to manifest its gifts out in the world, not in this darkened basement. Even if life outside was becoming increasingly insane—in the realm of a demented clown-president, the planet's thermostat clicking higher every day—I knew I'd gathered all the tools I needed. I wasn't healed, but I was healed enough.

The journey ended, as all journeys must. Later, as we sat in a circle to share our stories, I explained to the others what the symbol on the wooden token meant. As I told them about the trip I was about to take—*ha ha, the one to Hungary*—a woman decked out in a headscarf and a hippie sack dress piped up. "I have something for you," she said, poking around her collection of crystals and fishing out a clear piece of quartz. "Take this with you," she said, "and leave it there."

For a long moment, I wasn't sure what to do. Though I'd just wrestled with the consequence of carrying other peoples' baggage, I wasn't sure if I could refuse it. But now I remembered something a friend had said about my coming trip: "It's like you're bringing luggage, but you're taking it to leave there." I thanked the woman and tucked the crystal into my pocket.

Outside, the night air felt cool and refreshing. I powered on my phone and finally responded to Stacey's request: *I love you. Thank you for asking, and yes: Will you please come to Hungary with me?*

PART FIVE

Arrival

*Statue commemorating 2nd Transylvanian Hussar
Regiment, Castle District, Budapest*

37

Budapest, May 2019: Far beneath me, the earth unreels itself: A jagged moonscape, knifelike peaks hidden under a thick blanket of snow. Deep inside my red-eyed delirium I imagine flashes and eruptions below as the men of the *Gebirgstruppe*—the Austro-Hungarian mountain troops—hurl bullets and grenades and shit-filled cans at the Italian *Alpini*. That was a different century and a different mountain range—we're crossing Austria, not the Italian Alps—but the sight below me is no less awe-inspiring. As the crags recede behind us, I crane my neck for one last glimpse out the cabin window. Hungary looms ahead.

I am tired. No, scratch that: I am *fucking exhausted*. Much as I love traveling by air—*for how much longer, warming planet?*—I'm constitutionally unable to sleep on airplanes. And so by the tail-end of this, my third flight of the day, I'm hollowed-out and weary, my face pinched by tiredness. Even the excitement of this trip halfway around the world has faded. I want nothing more than to reach the cheap travelers' hotel that awaits me in Budapest, where I'll have two days alone before Stacey arrives.

As Lake Balaton rolls past to the south, excitement and dread entwine. I have barely any idea what I'm looking for, but thanks to some last-minute advice from a far-sighted friend, I'm bringing a new tool: A decent iPhone microphone, to help me capture audio snippets of my quest. Little do I know how crucial a role it will play.

Finally we burst from the high clouds and I see Budapest laid out like the child's pop-up book of my dreams. There's Margit Island, where my cousin Pal once showed me the ruins of an 800-year-old church; there's the National Assembly, Hungary's sprawling confection of a parliament building. There are the famous bridges—one, two, seven in all—spanning the great Danube, running north to south and separating Buda from Pest.

As we taxi to the gate I see how much has changed. The last time I was here—with my father, nearly twenty-five years ago—I thrilled at the sight of the aging Ilyushin and Antonov airliners parked on the tarmac. Now the airport looks less Hungarian and more European. I could be anywhere.

Almost. As I wait for my bag, the giant screen above the carousel flicks from an ad for a Hungarian dub of *Game of Thrones* ("*Trónok harca!*") to one in English: "Spíler Deli, serving modern and Jewish classics!"

Jewish classics? I'm dumbfounded. I mean, I didn't necessarily expect to see Arrow Cross graffiti on the walls, but I was on high alert for antisemitic messages. Back home I'd agonized over which books to bring, imagining hard-faced customs officers pawing through my luggage and finding *Masquerade*, Tivadar Soros' memoir. His son George, the Jewish philanthropist, is Public Enemy #1 here. I mean that literally: There are government billboards depicting his grinning, liver-spotted face, warning Hungarians not to be hoodwinked by a Jew. Fearful of being pegged a semitic provocateur, I'd left the book at home.

The ad for the restaurant throws me. Everything I've learned about this freshly sanitized Hungary suggests Jewishness is less tolerated than ever. But I can't read the language or understand the subtle (or not-so-subtle) messaging. Obviously the ad is aimed at foreign visitors, but what's the takeaway? That Hungary loves its Jews? Or just their food?

There are no customs officers on duty. I should have brought the book.

It's late spring and the air is already warm. As I step outside the terminal, it's the smells—diesel exhaust, low-grade cigarettes, cheap detergent—that remind me I'm in Eastern Europe. I find my bus and we lurch on our way. By the time I disembark, forty-five minutes later, I'm wrung-out and parched, fairly swaying from the hand straps. There's my hotel, a grubby building that looks like it's made from spare Ikea parts. I'm ready to drop off into sleep, but at the front desk the clerk frowns at her screen. "No, Mr. Lorinczi"—*they say my name so perfectly here!*—"there is no reservation under your name, nor are there any rooms available this week."

Furious, I pull out my phone. It's evening time here and midday in New York. The time difference allows for a couple of choice but impotent words with the Russian travel agent who booked, or rather didn't book my room. Then there's nothing to do but sit in the comically small lobby and wonder what the hell to do next. Cousin Pal is in Poland; he won't be back for a week. Poki, who would probably but not assuredly put me up, lives in the suburbs and is giving a presentation tonight. I'm on my own.

I pull out my phone again, hesitate for a moment, then dial.

"Baby!" says Julianna from 10,000 miles away. "Hi! Did you arrive okay?"

As soon as I hear her voice I'm flooded with gratitude. "Yeah, mostly. But can I get your Airbnb password?"

As I walk to catch another bus, my tiredness becomes hallucinatory. Now the wheel on my downmarket roller bag begins shredding itself into plastic hairs, emitting an occasional grating squeal. Could I have inspected it before leaving on my trip? *No I couldn't have, fuckface.* I am less than two hours in-country and things feel grim. But beneath my frustration is a subtler sensation: that I'm borne on unseen currents, spirited towards a purpose I can't yet see.

The next bus, a smaller and grimier one than the last, is nearly empty. A few rumpled-looking old people chat with the driver, woven plastic bags resting against their legs. The murmurs of words I recognize—*sajnálom; vicces; jó*—pierces me. Though I don't speak Hungarian, I grew up swaddled in its strange cadence. A doorway I stood next to but could never enter myself.

Now we're in Budapest proper. I thrill to the sight of the dingy parks, the rows of apartment blocks disappearing down curvilinear side streets. The light is fading, and in the shadows, their weathered facades come to life. Some are freshly painted and trim; others bear scars of the battle seventy-five years ago, when steel projectiles in their thousands bathed them in a metallic hail. Enfolded in the sounds of the language I'll never understand, I feel like crying. I am tender, a newborn. I feel the pull of ancestral tendons weaving through me but I can't understand where they lead, or why they've summoned me here.

Outside the streaky bus windows, pale ghosts flit by. There's Andor Klay, my childhood piano teacher's strangely reclusive husband, standing on a street corner in his eternal camel trench coat. I catch a glimpse of Laszlo Sokoly, our beloved family dentist. Seventeen years old in the summer of 1944, Laszlo was taken to a labor camp. The rest of his family stepped out of the filth of a cattle car onto the arrival ramp at Auschwitz. One sister was selected and walked to the right, towards the work camp. The others went left, to the showers.

Eventually I arrive at the Airbnb and collapse into a few hours of dreamless sleep. But when I awaken, at a quarter to two, it's not the weight of the duvet I feel but the crush of dread. Blinking myself awake, I'm awash in fear. The end—*the end of us, the species*—feels impossibly close. I am thousands of miles from my wife and daughter, chasing down a story—*mine? my shadowy father's?*—that quite possibly doesn't even exist. I've made a terrible mistake. If I had any doubts before, I'm certain now there's no market whatsoever for the book I am writing, or the one writing me.

For a long moment, home feels like a distant dream. Now that I'm here, I see how deep in I am, and I feel nakedly afraid. After a few minutes, a mantra comes to me: *Mutasd meg nekem.* Julianna looked it up before I left; it's Hungarian for "show me." I murmur it over and over, and eventually my heart rate slows.

Still, sleep won't come. In the dead of the Budapest night my quest feels murky and indistinct. I pray for it anyway: *I have done what you asked; I have travelled here with my ears, my eyes, and my heart open. What am I here for? Show me, show me, SHOW ME.*

38

Budapest, May 2019: Pale light filters in through the curtains. As I swim back up towards consciousness, the sounds of an unfamiliar city fill the room. After a bleary moment, I remember where I am, and my early checkout time. I hurriedly shower and repack my balky rolling bag. Then it's out onto the streets of Budapest, to do whatever it is I'm supposed to do here.

Starbucks; Burger King; Ecocafe Organic Coffee. The city feels slicker and less mysterious than it did during my last visit. Despite the jet lag, despite the dread I felt in the middle of the night, I sense the current that spirited me through yesterday's missed connections. It even has a visual cue: Fluffy cottonwood blooms, the same ones that drift through Portland every spring, rising and falling on the warm city air.

The first one I follow leads me down a side street and past a building with a neat blue placard: "Jewish Local History Collection." I stop, as if only now remembering that I'm Jewish, and my discomfort takes me by surprise. *Sure*, I figured there would probably be some Jewish stuff on this trip, but...on the very first morning? As I stand dumbly in the middle of the street, I feel that sensation on my chest again, the one that appeared when the DVDs from Deborah arrived. A gentle hand, neither holding me back nor urging me forward. I walk inside, hand the clerk a pile of brightly colored *forint* notes, ascend an elegant staircase, and step into a perfect restoration of a middle-class Jewish dwelling from a century ago. Aside from the docent, an older woman with exuberantly flouncy hair, I'm the only person here.

Here, right before my eyes, is a recreation of life in my grandparents' apartment. There's a gorgeous German-made piano complete with built-in candelabra, a massive wood stove clad in gleaming emerald tiles. I pause before the same kinds of toys my young father and aunt must have played with: ancient tin soldiers and cloth dolls, heavy leather-bound encyclopedias. A detail from my father's childhood pops up: He once told me that when he and Csupi were young, Muki insisted they take their meals with encyclopedias clenched between their elbows and ribs so as to demonstrate correct posture.

The exhibit is fascinating, but I feel a strange remove. The upright and observant Jews who lived here aren't my people. This idealized family kept Kosher—*two separate kitchens in an inner-city apartment, for god's sake!*—and they lived in the thick of Pest's Jewish Quarter, attending whichever of the three nearby synagogues best suited their aspirations. They didn't flee their tribe, imagining they might become Hungarians as easily as changing their address.

The tour complete, I linger to chat with the docent, who speaks excellent English. "The past feels very close here," I say. "Every street corner seems like it holds so many stories." She gives me a look I can't quite read. "A few months ago," she says, "I walked my father to the market down the street. He bought a bag of tomatoes, and then he pointed to the wall. He said: 'In 1944 there was a wooden box right there. I watched my mother surrender her last thing of value, her wedding ring, and put it in the box before we went inside'." That very first cottonwood bloom, I realize, led me directly to Budapest's former ghetto.

I thank the docent and leave, pausing on a bench to plot my course. If I still harbor any doubts as to the purpose of my visit, now a song plays from inside a nearby shop. It's Iz Kamakawiwo'ole singing "Somewhere Over the Rainbow." It's a famous recording, but I've only heard it once before, at the close of an ayahuasca ceremony. *All right,* I say out loud. *I get the goddamn hint. This is some kind of a medicine journey, isn't it?*

I spend the next few hours wandering aimlessly, blown from place to place with the fluffy white blooms. But my path is not random. I realize I'm being pulled closer and closer to the Danube, the city's aqueous heart. Some part of me wants to delay this moment, to prepare myself for the inevitable reckoning. And yet I'm already there, crossing Antall József Quay and stopping at the ancient footpath along the riverbank.

The water is a muddy aquamarine, fast-moving and opaque. More a living entity than a river. Now the Buda side sprawls before me in all its heart-stopping beauty. It's a thrilling sight, but it's a darker pull I feel: The echoes of what took place at this very spot, not so long ago.

In the closing months of 1944 the river became a graveyard, a cemetery with no headstones or visiting hours. In this cultured metropolis—a city of electric trams, cafés, and multi-level department stores—the banks of the Danube became an execution ground. It was the time of the Arrow Cross, when teenagers and middle-aged men with guns roamed the streets, hunting for Jews. They brought them here, to the river, lined them up on the banks and shot them down into the water. Not a few of them, not hundreds, but perhaps 15,000 of them. Lying awake at night, my fifteen-year-old father could hear what was being done in his country's name, right under the parliament building, night after night after sleepless night. How long would it be before they found him, too?

39

Budapest, May 2019: "Ooh, creamy gizzard stew! We're sharing, right?" Stacey and I are studying the menu at the unfortunately named "Gettó Gulyás," a bistro near the great Dohanyi Street synagogue. After a long-delayed flight, my sister's as tired as I was two days earlier. But as we take the last two seats at the counter and plates of food begin to arrive—none of them actually containing gizzards—a warm thrill courses through me. We are far from home in a place teeming with ghosts, but I feel a rising thrill of connection between us.

One thing's for certain: After two nights of broken sleep, I'm grateful for her company. Other than dinner the night before with Poki, there's only my conversation with the docent to count as human interaction. Actually, there was one other: Stopping at a convenience store for bottled water, I unleashed a cheerful "*Jó napot!*"—"Good afternoon!"—to the clerk, a bespectacled young man with downturned lips. He answered, without turning to face me, in English. "Oh come on," I said, flashing my winningest grin. "Is my Hungarian really that bad?" Now he looked up. "No," he said. "A Hungarian would never *greet* me.

He would just give me the water." We locked eyes. Not certain if he was kidding, I held my grin, but his eyes remained dead as a fish's. After a long moment I looked down, collected my change, and left.

Now, as my sister and I dig into plates of fried noodles and mushroom crepes, I feel the cobwebs of jet lag dropping away. Unlike me, Stacey anticipated it. "Within half an hour of making the reservation, I had a mild panic attack," she says. "It was a specific image: Waking up in a strange apartment by myself in the middle of the night, and feeling so alone and isolated and sad." It sounds eerily like what I've been experiencing the last two nights, and with this comes a quiet rush of connection. For all the years we've held each other at a distance, I'm certain there's no one else who understands this specific sadness in quite the same way.

"So," I say, "This trip kind of feels like a quest to me. To learn what really happened here. Honestly, I feel like I'm just following orders. It's eerie, but I'm just going with it. Anyway, yesterday I more or less stumbled into one of the major touchstones: The family apartment.

"I'd been walking around the Castle District for a few hours, and I was really beat," I went on. "So I walked back down the hill and hopped a tram back to Pest. As we rolled down Margit Boulevard I realized I was literally a block from the apartment. I thought I'd wait to visit it, but I felt the weirdest sensation: It felt like a hand on my chest."

I pause to study Stacey's reaction but she's quietly munching her chicken *paprikás*.

"So I got off and turned back toward Szász Károly Street," I say, and take a bite of tangily sour pickle. "And there it was. An ugly and crummy-looking building, honestly. But I'd been looking at it so long on Google Maps that it almost felt like I was walking onto the screen. There was the little TV repair shop and the staffing agency. And around the corner there's the little dirt plot where an Allied bomb took out our dad's living room. As I was wondering how to get in, a guy walked up and punched in the key code. I waited behind him until the last possible second and then slipped inside behind him. My heart was practically beating out of my chest!"

A server in a white shirt and vest brings a plate of flaky apple strudel. Stacey's still silent, so I press on.

"Walking the same hallways that Dad did, what—eighty years ago?—I really felt like I understood our family house in Washington better. How thick the walls felt, how quiet and protected it felt inside. I'm pretty sure Dad chose that house himself, while Rhonda stayed in Milwaukee with us. Can you imagine that? Anyway, I was probably inside the building for ten minutes before I got too nervous. I felt like I'd gotten what I came for. But here's the thing: I know the family were evicted in June of '44, when all of Budapest's Jews had to move to the yellow star houses. Then they ended up in a villa somewhere in the Buda Hills. The only thing is, I don't know *where*. Did Dad or Csupi ever tell you about this?"

Stacey is quiet, engaged in some internal calculus. It dawns on me that she not only doesn't share my enthusiasm, but maybe even resents it. It's only when the conversation—the monologue, really, because she's been silent for minutes—moves to the topic of our father's elusiveness that she finally responds.

"I wonder about the leaving piece," I say. "His always moving houses, or how he came back to Hungary constantly when we were kids."

"I don't think he would have seen it that way," she says. "You like to think he had a choice, but I don't think it's that simple. I think people's lives grow around them organically and they may not realize they're trapping themselves."

"Sure, but that doesn't make it untrue. He set up his life so he was constantly returning to Hungary. An unconscious choice is still a choice."

"I urge you to be cautious using that language," she says, with a force that surprises me.

"Duly noted," I say, and take another bite of apple strudel. I recognize the need for tact, but I'm spellbound by the sense that my efforts might finally be finding purchase. *What is she defending?*

The cloud dissipates as we finish our meal and stroll outside into the night. Soon we're at ease again, trying not to crack up as we duck into the lobby of a fancy hotel to use the bathroom. "This is pure Dad," says Stacey, fast-walking past the ornate marble-topped front desk: "Look like you belong here!"

"Um, isn't that the story of our lives?" I say, and we both break up into laughter again. We reach the Airbnb flat Stacey booked for us, and that night, for the first time since I've arrived, I sleep soundly and well.

40

Budapest, May 2019: Morning breaks bright under an untroubled sky. As I slip out of the apartment for my first espresso of the day, I feel a welcome bounce in my step. Pausing at the corner of Andrássy Boulevard, a thoroughfare so grand it's been declared a World Heritage Site, I snap a self-portrait. My face projects a surprisingly chiseled worldliness. I look like an actor, which is what I suppose I am: a man portraying a writer. But I can't place which actor. A few seconds later, I get my answer: Bruce Willis' likeness smirks out from a giant placard. He's hawking an energy drink called "Hell." It promises its users "Energy, Taste, Power!" *Yuck.*

Back at the flat, Stacey slumbers as I prepare a breakfast that would warm our father's heart: Plates of dense peasant bread and cheese, raw tomato and pepper, smoky paprika-hued *gyulai kolbász*, one of the many Hungarian salamis I remember from our youth. That our breakfast came from a dingy corner store—the tomatoes waxy and the bread's paper label baked right into the crust—only heightens its appeal.

Perhaps it's the espresso, but I'm electrified by the challenge of tracing my family's story. Shuffling through my notes, I review what I know of the timeline, starting with the arrival of the Germans in 1944. My father wrote about that day, a beautiful March morning not unlike this one:

> *I remember the day well: It was a Sunday, and the first thing we noticed was a number of German warplanes patrolling the skies over Budapest, occasionally buzzing low over the rooftops in a demonstration of strength. They need not have worried; the Hungarian army was by then so deeply penetrated by Nazi sympathizers that opposition was not a real possibility. I remember, also, watching on the street as by about noon the advance formations, light tanks and motorcycle troops, arrived in Budapest and with unerring, fearsome efficiency—seeming to know the city by heart—fanned out and secured all vital bridges and other points. They seemed tough, disciplined but somehow unthreatening.*

In one sense he's right: No one threatens the family with physical force, not yet. But almost immediately their liberties begin to vanish. Now Jews are not allowed to own cameras, so Muki surrenders his beloved Kodak. Jews are not allowed radios; away goes Grandma Helen's shortwave receiver. More proclamations follow, an endless line of black dominoes: Jews are no longer permitted to sit in cafés or eat in restaurants. They cannot attend movies or any other public performances. They cannot visit the public baths, own or even use telephones. They must surrender their automobiles. They no longer need them anyway, because they are forbidden to travel.

Back at the apartment, the family frets and paces the floor. Each morning brings a new shock, another piece of their lives vanishing into dust. In those sickening first days of April the walls fall in, one after another. My father and Csupi are expelled from school; Muki is dismissed from his job at the bank. Now all of them must wear the yellow star, which they must provide themselves. Food becomes scarce; the family are given yellow ration cards to match the loathsome hand-sewn badges. Each Jew's share is half that of a Gentile's.

Now a sign comes from above. On the morning of Monday, April 3rd, 1944, the city is subsumed by an unearthly wail pealing from dozens of sirens. Apartment block wardens join the overture, banging iron bars on railings, shouting across courtyards as the residents—ashen-faced, curious, or bemused—hustle down flights of stairs and into cellars marked with crude white-painted arrows. Now the ant-like activities of the city go mute, a deathly calm falling like the hush of first snow. The years of waiting are over. There is no more time to pretend this won't happen, can't happen, isn't happening. The war has arrived.

The puttering buses and electric trams have stopped; the broad squares are barren. There is nothing but sound: The undulating moan of the sirens reverberating across the lifeless boulevards. Then the overture fades, the people in the shelters tense and expectant, breath held in abeyance. Now come the kettledrums, faraway antiaircraft guns tracing the bombers' path as they approach. Distant, ominous *crrrumps.* Bowels clench; the body is helpless before the war drums. *Boom; boom; ba-boom.*

The sound leaps in volume as the guns along the Danube and on Gellert Hill come to life, big *flak* cannons heaving shells six miles high. The bombers are close now and the tempo quickens, the gunners on the ground throwing everything they have at them. The sound becomes frantic and hellish, smaller Bofors guns adding their incessant *thud-thud-thud-thud* to the cacophony. Below them, inside the shelters, the air grows thick and stale. Beads of sweat coalesce on lips and brows.

The guns fall silent but it brings no relief. The crews have only run for shelter because the bombs have begun to fall. The people huddled in the shelters can't see them, of course, but they hear piercing whistles, rising in pitch as they approach. Later, those who survive will call it "ear-shattering," a "nerve-breaking shriek." The sound bores into them, always seeming to come from directly overhead. Entire lifetimes compress into seconds as they wait for the impact. No one who has waited underneath the bombs will ever forget it.

In the shelters, everyone has forgotten to breathe.

The first explosions are reassuringly distant. Minutes pass by; perhaps they're only attacking Csepel Island? But now they come closer, the ground shaking as dust sifts down from ancient wooden rafters. Then: A deafening BOOM that rattles cans off shelves, shelves off walls, the lights flickering, the sound of breaking glass, a shouted curse. The earth lurches. The startled groans of the elderly, the crying of an infant, somebody farting, the terrified sounds and smells of humans stuffed into musty basements, all wondering when the roof will give way.

For my family, the roof does not give way, not yet. They will survive this raid, and the ones that follow it, nearly every day and every night. But a different roof gives way: The next morning, a decree is read over the radio. Because the attack was obviously orchestrated by the Jews, fifteen hundred of them must surrender their apartments. It is only a taste of what is to come. Soon, all Budapest's Jews must move to the yellow star houses, apartments requisitioned to concentrate Budapest's nearly 200,000 Jews. But why? Suddenly a new word is on everyone's lips: *Deportation.* But…to where?

Inside the yellow star houses, entire families cram into a single room, dozens of souls stuffed into apartments designed for a small family. They are only allowed out a few hours a day, but this no longer offers relief. *"Jews are not served here,"* read signs outside the shops they once frequented. It's not just the bombs hurtling from above they must fear but the people on the ground, the guards now posted at each bridge and major intersection, the neighbors who report them for not wearing the star, or approach them in the street to leer silently in their faces, knock their hats off their heads, launch a gob of spit directly in their eyes. Suddenly, nowhere is safe.

I look up from my laptop, my heart racing. It's 2019, not 1944. My sister is stirring. As I fix her one of those weird pod coffee things, I turn over the little I know and the lot I don't. I know *when* the family left the apartment on Szász Károly, but not *where*. There were nearly 2,000 yellow star houses. For all I know, I've already walked by it. I could ask Aunt Csupi, but these days her stories are mostly limited to a few greatest hits playing on endless loop. The trail has gone cold.

The question nags at me, but it's time to leave. Stacey and I walk towards a tram. We're headed to the Buda Hills to meet Kata, the daughter of one of our father's closest friends. It's a gorgeous day and the Margit Bridge is jammed with sightseers. Me? I'm held in a reverie, caught in some in-between time. Mixed in with the happy crowds, I imagine the hunched and downtrodden figures of my family, laden with overstuffed suitcases and trunks. Where they're headed, I have no idea. Neither, I realize, do they.

41

Budapest, May 2019: As the bus chugs past stately villas and gated compounds, the landscape seems eerily familiar. I realize

I've been here before, during that mournful farewell trip with my father. As we draw closer to Normafa Park, I gather up my slim recollections of Kata. It's been fifteen years since I last saw her. Now tiny pebbles of memory rattle inside me: her father Ivan's handsome, fox-like face; his well-fitted grey suits and French silk ties. The same uniform as my father's, but tailored for a decidedly leaner body.

Stacey and I disembark at a crowded parking lot and then we see her: A striking woman, dark hair framing a softer version of her father's face.

We embrace, and as we walk through sun-dappled paths and rolling meadows together, she tells us why she returned to Hungary.

"Well, you know my father Ivan was here," she says. "But he died."

"Yes, I remember that," says Stacey. "I'm so, so sorry."

"It never should have happened. A doctor bungled a routine procedure; he used a drainage tube that probably wasn't even disinfected. They transferred him to a different hospital and operated on him. Even though he wasn't getting better, they tried to send him home! He was perfectly healthy before all this, and a month later he was dead."

Ivan died a few years after my father, but Kata's hurt is as raw as if it happened last week. I think of the expert medical care my father received back in the States, the choices he could make even up to the final days of his life. Ivan was in every way my father's equal and his peer. He just got sick in the wrong place.

As we trudge up the steep hill to Erzsébet-kilátó, the 19th-century lookout tower overlooking the park, Kata rattles off a litany of the ways Hungary is the wrong place for Jews like her. "I think Hungarians are completely antisemitic, even those who don't know what a Jew looks like. That's why Orbán can put Soros on those banners everywhere and people believe he's our enemy."

"The other day I saw a poster with a painting of Viktor Orbán holding a little girl," I say. "It was done up in '70s Socialist style; it looked weirdly retro."

"Yes!" says Kata, a hard edge to her voice. "It's not subtle at all. You know those round news posts you see on corners, and the posters that say 'Brüsszel'? That's a taunt to the E.U., saying we won't accept their quotas of Syrian refugees. Only there *aren't* any quotas. It's all made up to help rally people behind Orbán, and it's working!"

"I remember something my father told me after the Wall came down. 'Just wait,' he said. 'Hungary will have fifteen years of freedom and expansiveness, and then it will go right back to how it was, only worse.' I'm glad he's not here to see how right he was."

"I remember how dismissive Irene was of Hungary," says Stacey. "She could barely conceal her contempt for this place, her disdain of our dad's heritage and food." She trails off for a moment. "Now that I'm actually here, I wish I could convey my enthusiasm to him."

Kata doesn't share my sister's interest in Hungarian food. "Grease and meat," she says flatly. It's touching to see her, to feel our ancestral connection. But her anxiety is rampant and hot, and there's no place to steer the conversation that doesn't trip hidden land mines. Like the one about my stepmother, Irene.

"You know, I interned at your father's law firm. One afternoon I called to check on Irene, when she was already very sick with the cancer. When I asked after her health, Irene took the phone from her ear and, without covering it up, called out sarcastically to your father: 'George, Kata is calling and she wants to know how I'm doing!' It was so humiliating. I just froze."

I let out an involuntary gasp. If nothing else, I know my memories of Irene aren't wrong.

We ramble deeper into the park, admiring the breathtaking sight of Budapest laid out below. But Kata has gone quiet. Every avenue seems to lead inevitably back to loss, to hopelessness in the face of overwhelming odds. She's a wild animal pacing in loops, refusing to submit to simple compassion. When Kata tells me she more or less abandoned her legal career, I feel an uncomfortable pang. I'd stepped away from a promising food-writing career in San Francisco, back in the '90s. What convinced the children of two self-made Jewish strivers that this world offered them no home?

42

Budapest, May 2019: The day waning, Stacey and I take our leave and head back down to the city. I'm looking forward to tonight's dinner: Stacey's found a restaurant so old it's possible our grandfather Muki ate here, back when it had just opened and he was an officer *kadett* at the Ludovica Academy. We walk in and step back in time: A book-lined dining room; dark parquet floors; white-aproned servers. "I hope this is good," says Stacey. "What's the saying? 'The best meals begin with hunger'?"

"I think it's: 'The best meals begin with ethnically motivated hatred.' Plus, it's going to be *great!* Did you see how the server put down my beer with an artful little spiral?"

Stacey's eyes have a familiar gleam: "Are you sure that doesn't mean 'Meet me in the bathroom in ten minutes'?"

"Please," I sigh. "In Hungary, that only takes place after the dessert course."

We reminisce about the last time we were in Europe together, when our father was dying. "That was brutal," says Stacey, but her tone is light. There's no pain to hold on to now. The pole stars of loss have faded, and in their place are memories of meals with relatives and friends and our father's funny little quirks, like his obsession with rabbits. It's only now that I can acknowledge how much has changed since he died.

"I remember how closed and self-protected I felt then. It's funny, the time around his death was this great opening, but once he was gone and we returned to D.C., it all fell apart."

"That's very true," she says, pausing to graze off the charcuterie plate. "Oh, that's a good pickle! A little sweet, a little vinegary…a well-balanced pickle!"

We fall quiet as more food arrives, including a miniature cauldron of the inevitable *gulyás*. Here it's a simple and heart-warming soup, not the bland and starchy stew I remember from school lunches in the '70s. And a dish that will recur again and again throughout my trip: A duck or goose leg braised and then crisped into rich submission, always served with cabbage and potatoes smashed with golden fried onions. It strikes me, somehow, as being akin to my family's Jewishness: It's just the way it's always been, and there's no possibility of it ever being anything but. No wonder our father left.

The talk turns to our afternoon with Kata, how her Jewishness seems like an inescapable weight. "You know, I grew up thinking my mom was Jewish and my dad was Unitarian," she says. "I didn't even know. I also thought the world was like 50% Jewish."

"Exactly! Doesn't that tell you something about the power of illusion?"

"No. What I find interesting with Dad is that he was going to come to America and work his ass off. He was going to execute everything flawlessly. He would be the best American and the best lawyer…."

"Down to the Pierre Cardin silk ties. But what everything left unsaid, like his Jewishness?"

"He was definitely *sui generis*, self-made," she answers carefully. "I don't think he was a pretender."

"I think it was happening on a level so deep he was no longer even aware of it. It was a survival strategy; he and our grandparents were utterly cast out of society. That's why I'm here: To understand how he was forced into this mode, and what that unconscious code-switching passed on to me."

I bring up his elementary school years, and how once—after suggesting that the English and French might honor their war dead the same way the Austro-Hungarians did—he was very nearly expelled. After this, how his classmates pushed him to the playground dirt day after day, taunting him for his treason and his Jewishness. I leave out the part about his classmates essentially sexually assaulting him; instead, I bring up a word I'd recently learned.

"Have you ever heard the word *zsidózni?*" I ask. "I learned it from a novelist who's the son of a Hungarian Jew. It means 'to Jew.' As in: 'To ostracize, shame, or otherwise assault someone in the manner one would a Jew.' What do you think that did to him?"

She doesn't know any of this.

I'm incredulous. "Then there were the blood infections he suffered as a young boy; he was paralyzed by the second one. Csupi told me they got a phone call to come down to the hospital because he was going to die. Can you imagine how terrifying and isolating that was?"

Her face remains blank. The father I knew and the one she did seem to bear little resemblance to one other.

"I see where you're going with this," Stacey finally responds. "That he made up stories to mask the more painful real ones. But myth making is a part of so many self-made people's lives. I mean, there's that bit about the French Foreign Legion."

At this we both explode into laughter. After leaving Hungary in 1946, our father arrived in Paris with a letter of introduction to the music conservatory. Apparently, after a humiliating few weeks, he briefly considered joining the Foreign Legion. "I can see him struggling up a sand dune under a rucksack, drenched in sweat," Stacey giggles. "It's a scene straight out of *Crock!* But all that aside, I didn't experience the mythmaking so much. I mean, the Army part: He told me that he was in basic training in the States but never made it to Korea…."

"Not what he told me; he said he served in Korea. After he died, I wrote the VA for his military records. No Korea."

Stacey is quiet for a moment. I sense the levers and gears at work inside, but her face remains unreadable. For a long moment, I don't know how she'll respond, whether she'll shut me down again or allow the door to crack open a hair further.

"I know you have a hypothesis, and it makes for a more entertaining story, but…." She trails off. "I'm not saying that because I'm protecting him; I'd prefer the tall tale-telling side. It would be super amusing, but I don't know that it's him."

"But you have evidence of the tall tales, and you weren't told the others. We were told different things."

"I was told the truth! I think of him as a fundamentally honest person."

"That's called implausible denial. Those projections are the creations of a fundamentally honest person put in an impossible situation, in which he's lost all his agency, his power, his identity. When he told me he commanded a tank in Korea…."

"Did he *really* tell you that?," she groans. "Are you sure this isn't a *Tintin* plot?"

"Yes! You remember how he loved reading those books with me! But they're this parallel version of Europe. Everything is sanitized and clean. The continent isn't starving and ruined. Those books are a projection, and that's how I see his stories, too. They're versions of the story in which he didn't lose everything."

A tiny snifter of apricot *palinka* arrives. Even more than the quiet crackle of flame caressing my tongue it's the scent that takes me back. I am ten years old again, standing in the little service bar off the back staircase, using my nose to explore the worlds contained in those glimmering bottles. Before I started drinking them to erase myself, a couple of years later.

Stacey is thoughtful. "As his last child, and his best child, I think I got the best of him. He had unburdened himself by that point."

"The genes had…weakened by that point," I reply in a professorial tone, but she pushes on.

"I mean he was the most self-confident then. He'd checked all the boxes. So I wonder if there's a relationship between his status in the world and his truthfulness. Maybe he didn't feel the need to embellish as much as he had."

"I think so. But that's a funny thing, the success piece. Deborah took a graduate class with Elie Wiesel. At one point, she made a reference to our father being a 'famous Hungarian lawyer,' and she saw Wiesel's eyes widen. In that moment she realized our father wasn't quite the person he'd presented himself as."

"What'd Wiesel know?"

"He was a Romanian Jew, born at the same time, who underwent many of the same experiences and moved in the same circles. Dad projected this sort of penetration of the upper ranks, a status that maybe wasn't exactly borne out by reality. There's something else Deborah told me. Just days after Dad died, Ruth—his first wife—sent her a copy of a letter he'd written in the late '40s. It was an official request for reparations on account of his having been held in a Romanian prison camp." I pause to let the implications of this fabrication sink in. "Of course, the fact that she shared this with her on the occasion of his death says a lot about Ruth…."

"*Fascinating!* The sneaky little bastard! That strikes me as such a Jewish scam. Not to be too racist."

"Um, let's let that one slide. It's just…*that's* not the father we knew, right? Can you see what I'm getting at?"

We finish our dessert and step back out into the cool night air. Later, back at our flat, I decide I've gone long enough without hearing Julianna's voice. I duck outside, check the time—it's 1pm in Portland—and dial her number.

"Hi love!" she says. She sounds ebullient at the sound of my voice, and I feel a warm thrill in my chest. "How are you doing?"

"I'm great! My time with Stacey has been surprisingly good. Maybe a little static the first day or two, but not now. The food is helping; tonight we ate at this beautiful place near the river, an old-fashioned menu with dishes like beef *tartaré*, grilled *foie gras*, that sort of thing."

"Is she interested in the quest part of your trip?"

"Honestly, no. But I feel like something shifted tonight. Maybe it's not a wholehearted embrace, but something's opening up. Like maybe she's wondering if our father was more of an iceberg than she realized. But she doesn't want to dig. I guess that's all on me."

"Baby, keep going. You're right where you're supposed to be and you're right on time."

We say goodnight and I go back upstairs to bed. But an uncomfortable twinge stirs inside me, and sleep is once again elusive. The feeling from a few days before, when I heard that song from ayahuasca, is even stronger. This *does* feel like a medicine journey: fractal clues and memories that aren't even mine rising up and then vanishing just as quickly. Everything is telling me to use what I've learned in all those medicine experiences: to close my eyes and see. Yet I cling to facts and certitude, the hope that a more or less linear story will magically appear before my eyes. If I thought that coming here would feel like a triumph, I was very much mistaken. I've traveled halfway around the world to find my father, and yet he feels farther away than ever.

43

Budapest, May 2019: The next days pass as if in a dream. Later, it's the sounds I capture with my new microphone that will jog my memory: the clinking of plates and glasses, the murmurs of Hungarian in the background. Searching for the dishes our grandmother prepared, my sister and I navigate a landscape of forgotten flavors. We taste a never-ending array of pickles: cabbage salads, vinegary peppers, crunchy cucumbers. We sample our way through crisp breaded cutlets, garnished with thick hand-rolled noodles or parsley-flecked potatoes. No pastry shop is too humble to pass up, especially when there are old-fashioned cookies on offer, encrusted not with sugar but a dark rime of honey. We pause in the café of the magnificent Gellért Hotel for the namesake roulade, a sheer chocolate robe encasing cake, pastry cream, sour cherries and bits of brittle. Reading frames hang nearby, to protect one's hands from newsprint. Behind us, an older gentleman in a suit and tie plays Lizst on a baby grand.

When we were children, the foods of Hungary were something of a joke in our household. Following our stepmother's lead, we turned up our noses at the archaic pleasures of sour cream and chicken fat. Now these flavors guide us down ancient pathways of memory. I can't recall which of those floating white blossoms leads us to the tiny lunchroom off Klauzál Square, the heart of Budapest's Jewish ghetto. But as soon as we step inside, we know we're in the right place. Framed photographs plaster the walls, clear plastic tablecloths cover red-and-white plastic ones. The owner—a man in rumpled headwaiter's whites who looks to be in his early 120s—tallies up diners' meals on an '80s-vintage tabletop calculator, each slice of white bread and glass of self-serve seltzer accounted for.

This is the food I remember, or forgot that I did: Tomato-braised cabbage leaves enfolding a filling of rice-studded meat, a tangle of tender sauerkraut on top. Tiny hand-pinched liver dumplings bobbing in milky broth, slices of meatloaf surrounding a startled eye of hard-cooked egg in the middle. I've seen this magic trick only once before: In the cool subterranean kitchen of our home in Washington, where I goggled in wonder as Csurka served us her own version. *How did she put the egg inside the meatloaf?*

Stacey remembers those meals too, and as we eat and talk I learn more about the woman who prepared them. I forgot that our grandmother had a softer side, taking Stacey to pick mulberries in the vacant lot next to our house, teaching her old-fashioned card games like gin rummy. I'm heartened to learn that the memory of our grandmother might be a warm glow instead of a cold void.

My entrée arrives: boiled beef with sorrel sauce. It's the very apex of unglamorous, and I'm not sure what compelled me to order it: Hunks of plain stringy beef, a clump of potatoes, the sorrel—an herb that, raw, delivers a bracingly tart burst—cooked here into a pool of thick, sweet olive drab. It's also unaccountably delicious, the kind of cheap diner food I secretly love. As I eat, the sounds of clinking silverware and other diners' conversations surround me in synesthetic grace. At a table behind us, an older woman croons "Jó, jó, Gyurikám!" I recognize the words: "Good, good, dear George!" I've heard this phrase a thousand times, but not since I was a boy: It's what my father's friends and family called him.

I hadn't realized it, but much of this food is explicitly Jewish, subsumed into the pantheon of Hungarian cooking just like that of the nation's other bogeymen, the Romani. Hungary hates the people but loves their music and food. At dinner with Poki a few nights before, he'd explained with a sheepish smile that when a bite of food goes down wrong it's called "swallowing the gypsy way."

In America, I rarely pause to ponder my Jewishness. Here, I'm watchful for threats that fail to appear. The walls aren't spray-painted with Arrow Cross graffiti; the grand Dohány Street synagogue is a popular tourist attraction. If my face gives me away, I'm not aware of it. I'm merely another American, bumbling my way through Budapest's astonishing beauty. I recognize there's a part of me still seeking confirmation of my outsiderness. But I do not belong, or unbelong, any more here than anywhere else. I am merely who I say I am.

Perhaps that's why our friends here seem slightly wary of me. I ask uncomfortable questions about my father, a man they revered. Eventually, I'll ask enough of those questions to piece together a portrait of my father's alternate life here: One in which he is a beloved *bácsi*—a literal or honorary uncle—bearing presents from America, hosting lavish dinners and swims at the hotel pool. But whether it's my line of questioning or some other part of my nature, our friends gravitate towards Stacey instead. She's always breezed through the world borne on her attractiveness and charm, her diction burnished at an Ivy League school, where she hobnobbed with Rothschilds. She doesn't ask troubling and impertinent questions, has no desire to rouse the ghosts. I can't help but feel a twinge of envy, even as I betray myself by asking more of those probing questions.

"Where do we go next?" asks Stacey as she spears a pickle. "This has been one of the trips of my life; I think we should do this on a regular basis!"

"I agree. This *has* been an incredible trip, and I'm glad beyond words that you came. But not back here." For all the unexpected joy of our time here, it's unease I feel. Stacey's been here nearly a week; tomorrow she'll fly back home. The dread that encircled me those first nights hasn't dissipated, but waits patiently for me. I sense I'm at a threshold of some kind, and the twinge of anxiety ramps up in response.

As Stacey and I finish our lunch, it's nearly closing time. When we ask the server if there's any dessert left, she strides to the kitchen and returns with a plate of what looks very much like a mistake: A pile of sugar-dusted cake crumbs nestled against a pool of apricot jam. "*Kaiserschmarrn*," she announces. Thrown together or not, it's stupidly delicious. "I hate to be maudlin," says Stacey between mouthfuls, "but this is like eating a hug!"

"Um, there's something very wrong-sounding about that," I say, but she's right. Our father, our grandparents, *their* grandparents must have eaten and loved this very same dish. It's enough to banish the currents of dread, at least for the moment.

That evening, Stacey and I enjoy a final dinner in the Buda hills with Kata and her rambunctious four-year-old, Poki, and his lovely wife and daughter. I'm careful not to push the conversation where it doesn't want to go, and the night blooms into something expansive and warm. Somehow the story of how Poki's father became my grandparents' doctor morphs into a joke about how Poki met his wife standing in line at a post office, or the origins of my grandmother's famous *rácz-ponty*, the Serbian-style baked carp that, truth be told, no one but my father actually liked. The only friction comes when I mention the restaurant my father took me to on our last trip. I recall the way his eyes widened as he described their sweet *túrógombóc* dumplings: "They tremble," he said, his own voice trembling, "as they bring them to the table!"

Just as I hoped, the room erupts as though I've tossed a grenade on the table. "Yes, that is Náncsi néni!" says Kata, only to be cut off by Poki: "No, you must try the ones at Rosenstein...." "Yes, but Ildikó's mother makes them better!" The argument ricochets from English to Hungarian and back again, and I grin from ear to ear. *This is how the story should end*, I think, sitting at the dinner table with our ancestral friends, basking in the buried treasure our father left for us here, a web of friendships that stretches across generations. It's been a long time, I realize, since I was held in the goodwill of people who loved me before I was even born.

Stacey will leave the following day. I'll embrace her in the thin morning light of Deák Ferenc Square, recognizing that we've crossed some threshold together. In the unfamiliar air of this ancient city, reveling in the gifts our father so artfully prepared for us, there are no wounds to exhume, no grievances begging payback. There is more richness and love in my life than I ever believed possible, and all I had to do to claim them was to show up.

And with this, my journey truly begins.

PART SIX

Descent

Budapest, 1945. Photo by Lissák Tivadar, courtesy Fortepan

44

Washington D.C., July 1993: *Some weeks have passed since I wrote the last chapter in this narrative; I would like to think that this is mostly due to summertime and lazy days. This is true, but not the whole truth. As I come nearer to the war and the terrible times we lived through, I am more and more reluctant to continue. To write about those times requires a systematic gathering of one's thoughts and memories; an exercise, I now realize, I have not engaged in during all those long years which have since passed.*

I would not have thought that in that distance, and even the very comfortable and happy circumstances in which I live and write this, the process would be so painful. The events I am about to describe—and I must, if this history should tell you the central events of our family's life—are so horrendous and awful to recall that I know that I cannot relate them with the impact and immediacy I would want. Even in my own mind, these recollections are at the same time vivid as yesterday and utterly unbelievable.

45

Budapest, May 2019: The moment I hear the buzzer's raspy sigh I leap up, bound down three flights of stairs, race through the foyer, throw open the great wooden doors to the apartment block and there he is: My cousin Pal. Tall and lanky, stony face crinkled by a resting expression of bemusement. He looks, I realize, not unlike our shared forebear Uncle Desző, Csurka's connection at the bank. It's been two years since I last saw him and twenty before then, but within seconds our conversation has fallen into its usual pattern: Unforced and absurdist mockery.

"Pal!" I say, "You look…well, not so good. But it's nice of you to finally show up."

"Yes, well, the border guards didn't want to let me back in," he says, taking a drag from his eternal cigarette. "They were afraid I'd be corrupted by 'some American asshole.' Do you know who they were talking about?"

I'm moving to Pal's flat for the remainder of my stay. Fortunately for my disintegrating luggage, it's only a few minutes' walk from my Airbnb. As we round the corner, Pal points to the street sign reading *Falk Miksa Utca.* "You know our family sheltered here," he says, "during the time of the yellow star houses, right?"

I stop dead in my tracks. "Wait. You're serious? This whole time I've been trying to find out what happened after they were kicked out of Szász Károly. And it was right here, under my nose?"

Pal shrugs and lights another cigarette.

"Do you know about the villa in Buda?" I ask. "And what about the time Muki was arrested?" He shoots me a mournful look. "I don't know. Eventually, of course, you will need to call Csupi."

I sigh. Csupi is Pal's grandmother, and—no surprise—their relationship is sometimes fraught. Pal can do nothing right, it seems: Always choosing the wrong girl, the wrong haircut, the wrong career. Still, once or twice a year he makes the twelve-hour train journey to Switzerland to check on her. Somewhat guiltily, I haven't even told her I'm in Europe. If I did, there'd be no getting out of a time-consuming detour to visit her. Pal is right: If anyone knows the answers to these decades-old riddles, it's Csupi. But she's a lockbox without a key. Once she launches into one of her well-worn stories, it's nearly impossible to redirect her. Still, she's my only hope. No one else knows what happened in those chaotic months after the Germans arrived, when everything fell apart.

We arrive at Pal's building, an Art Deco apartment block a few hundred feet from the Margit Bridge. He'd described it as "the best spot in the city," but then again his humor tends towards the ironic. Whatever else it is, it'll be my home for the next three weeks. Unholstering a weighty key ring, he selects one and opens the great wooden door: "After you, please."

Inside the air is dark and cool, and for a moment I feel as though I've stumbled into a tomb. As my eyes adjust I see that the cavernous lobby was once grand, with fantastic sculpted sconces and metal placards stamped with the names of former residents. Like Budapest itself it's weathered, shabby, and elegant all at once. A set of pale stone stairs leads upwards, but we opt for the rickety elevator instead.

Pal's flat is a one-bedroom, as ageless and worn as the lobby: Herringbone parquet, leaky radiators, a tiny bathtub. The electricity only works in half the apartment, and the appliances—a creaky electric stove and a rusting washing machine—are not to be trusted. One faucet doesn't work at all. The shelves are crammed with books and an antique turntable, and my bed is a rickety couch in the living room. But I love it at first sight. And first smell: The aroma of old and well-loved books permeates the place, as does the doggy odor of Lili, the wolfhound mutt

Pal found as a puppy in the countryside, only days after his beloved hound had succumbed to cancer.

Pal ducks out to the tiny and visibly crumbling balcony to smoke. I follow him; a sprawling view of Pest stretches out before us. As I apply a dab of an artisanal botanical fragrance I brought to my wrist, Pal crinkles his nose: "Ah! A defense against women?" I scowl to keep from cracking up.

Somewhat guiltily, I've given in to my half-hearted smoking habit, reasoning it will help me fit in. Everyone smokes here, despite the gruesome government-mandated stickers depicting grieving orphans, lonely headstones, and closeups of tongue cancers. One afternoon I pass a family who've paused on the sidewalk to chide their son, who's struggling to light his smoke. They're not razzing him for smoking, but for lagging behind. He looks no older than thirteen.

That evening, Pal and I share another meal my father would love: Dense black bread, tinned fish, pickled cucumbers and shredded cabbage. It's so good to be with him, to ponder the quirks of fate that have led us to live parallel lives half a world apart. I've never needed to explain myself to him, to soften my black humor or the essential sense of separateness that animates it. We are both outsiders of a sort, him torn from his peers by a childhood bout with cancer. Like me, Pal's love of people is at war with his pessimism regarding our species. Now, as our talk inevitably turns to the ruination of the planet, I see that his hopelessness is running rampant.

"You know, I own that farmhouse in Lókút," he says, pausing to light a cigarette. I knew he'd bought a small parcel of land a few miles north of Lake Balaton. "We have yoga retreats, art festivals, these kind of things. Many environmental activists come."

I can feel more than hear the anxiety in his voice, and I brace myself. "They are very pessimistic; there is no hope. Once the tundra begins to melt and release carbon, they say, we are done. The media will not report it because it's too frightening."

"I know," I say, trying to keep my voice level. *Do I?* I can barely acknowledge it myself. Inside, I feel the dread of the past week finally finding purchase in my body, threading its way into muscle and bone with practiced ease. For a long moment, it's all I can do to keep my composure. For the rest of the meal we make small talk.

"Well, I'm off," says Pal. "There is a retreat at Lókút this weekend. Don't burn the place down, and I'll see you on Monday."

We embrace and then he's gone. The heavy security gate clangs shut behind him and I hear the metallic scrape of the key. Now it's just me in the dark apartment. Me and the ghosts.

46

Budapest, May 2019: I awaken to pale light outside. It's dawn, finally, and I'm grateful. As I rub my eyes and brush off tufts of Lili's hair, memories of my sleepless night drift back to me.

As I tossed and turned on the threadbare couch, the sounds of the city—drunken conversations, the mewling of an elderly and evidently deaf cat—offered no relief. Beyond the courtyard I saw the lights of Nyugati station, where Gestapo officers trolled for fleeing Jews in the first days of the occupation. And beyond that, across the Carpathians and the flat wastes of Russia, the tundra, its frozen lifeblood melting out minute by pitiless minute. As the hours dripped by, I toggled between impatience and anxiety. I knew that relief would only come once I turned towards my fear, but still I resisted. *I am in charge*, I raged. *I am here to write my story, and you cannot stop me.* But Spirit offered no response. Eventually, I grasped a few wretched hours of sleep.

I want more than anything to hear Julianna's voice, but there's no relief here, either: It's midnight in Portland. And so I stretch and rise from the couch instead. Today's line of inquiry: The Labor Service.

After Deborah's offhand remark in Laramie, I'd added the Labor Service—the *Munkaszolgálat*—to my list of research topics. I found it darkly fascinating; in a sense, it was Hungary's home-grown Holocaust. Marketed as a wholesome program to employ those deemed unfit for military service, its true aim was to separate Jews, communists, foreign nationals, and other enemies of the state from their communities. The men cleared forests and built roads, returning home after a three- or four-month stint. In fact, my grandparents' physician, Dr. Endre Szántó—Poki's father—documented his service in 1940 with his Kodak Retina, the best amateur camera of the day. He captured six hundred quietly compelling photographs and filled three notebooks with his observations, all written in blotchless fountain pen. I'd seen many of them myself when I visited Poki's apartment.

In this first phase, the Labor Service was brutal but it wasn't murderous. Soon this would change. In 1942, Hungary's doomed Second Army trudged east towards Stalingrad with roughly 50,000 Jewish laborers in tow. The men were chronically underfed and often forced to sleep in the open; before long they were wracked by typhus and dysentery. As the Hungarians came into contact with the Red Army, the laborers began to be expended like unwanted playthings: Made to clear minefields with sticks; forced to bury fallen soldiers under Soviet gunfire; beaten or starved or deliberately frozen to death in the howling brutality of the Russian winter. After the Army's crushing defeat, it's estimated that fewer than one in seven laborers made it home alive. This is how my father's Uncle Miklós—the chief engineer of the sugar plant, the one who treated him to that heart-pounding ride at the controls of the beet-hauling locomotive—met his fate. "The circumstances of his death," my father wrote, "do not bear thinking about."

In 1942 my father was thirteen, and thus shielded from conscription. But by the summer of 1944, the Labor Service was running out of warm bodies. That's when my father received the official notice to report for duty.

> *I will never forget the pained look on my mother's*
> *face as we said goodbye that morning, or the shattered*
> *voice of my father, who told me he did not know how*
> *to advise me when I asked him if I should report or not.*

Again, the past and present zip neatly together. I know what happened next, because my father took me there himself on my last visit to Budapest: That quiet alleyway in Pest.

I remember looking through an archway into a courtyard with whitewashed walls. There was little to place us in time; come nightfall, I could easily imagine the place bathed in torchlight. But for the car and driver behind us, we are alone. The decades flicker by as if borne on woolly moths' wings: 2019; 1996; 1944. Now I see a long line of young men, hundreds of them just like my father, all waiting to see what happens next. They shift uneasily on the cobblestones, one foot to the other, under the hot summer sun.

I see two fathers. There is the old man standing beside me, sixty-seven years old, the end of his life only months away. And there is the young one, the one standing in line, just fifteen years old. He has not yet begun to live, has done nothing with his life, has not lain with a warm lover by his side, red-faced and spent in the cool of a grassy meadow. Nothing has even happened and he is being asked to decide his own fate with no guidance, no instruction manual, no clue.

My father stands there with the others, grasping desperately for a sign. He looks up to where the line snakes through a doorway in the building's flank. With no fanfare, no parting of the clouds or sudden thunderhead breaking above, he recognizes that what awaits him there is death. That if he walks through that doorway and signs his name on the ledger, his life is over. Without a word, my father turns and steps out of the line.

A startled murmur arises behind him, but he doesn't turn to face it. No one stops him; no one follows. He walks to the archway and keeps going. To somewhere, to *anywhere* but what awaits him here. He keeps walking, faster and faster, gait steady beneath a jackhammering heart.

Everyone who will survive what's to come must pass through an infinite number of gates. You take a left turn into a checkpoint instead of walking one block further. A bomb falls on one building instead of another. You rise to add a dash of salt to your macaroni just as a shell bursts outside the cellar window. But if it must be narrowed down to a single instant, a shiny silver capsule of time, this is the moment my father turns towards himself, and thus towards me. He does something braver and bolder and more frightening than anything I can imagine. This is the moment he makes me and my life—be it squanderous or blessed—possible as well.

Now I remember something else he said. That looking at the line of boys standing in the hot sun, he saw only sheep. That this turning towards himself was also a turning away, a separation from the Jews suddenly become bleating livestock. Is this the place he cuts that umbilical cord? If so, he does a lousy job of it. It will continue to trail after him, an angry red appendage that will never fully heal.

Nothing much had happened on these anonymous cobblestones, and everything. My father and I turned and got back in the car.

47

Budapest, July 1944: Time speeds up. My father feels a great swell of relief and excitement. After the years of mounting dread he's finally in motion, learning how to swim in fast-moving waters. A plan begins to coalesce.

First he'll need a new identity. Csupi's boyfriend, a charismatic but unstable neighborhood fixer named Andor, knows people: Printers and painters, good with their hands. Just like that, with a forged birth certificate, my father becomes Catholic. Soon these forgeries will number in the tens of thousands, and the authorities will inspect them with ever-increasing scrutiny. But for the moment, it's something to which he can cling.

Next: A place where he can hide in plain sight. There's a civil defense organization called *Légoltalmi Liga*, or "LEGO." During the air raids, LEGO crews man ambulances, enforce the blackout, fight fires. Because Jews are not allowed to serve, it follows that no member of LEGO can be Jewish. And so my father, all of fifteen, walks to a LEGO unit in Buda and volunteers. How the duty officer fails to notice my father's Jewish-looking features, I'll never know. But thanks to his forged scrap of paper, now he has the perfect disguise: A uniform.

My father is given a cursory first-aid course and assigned to the three-man crew of a military ambulance: Grey, with a large red cross painted on its side. Most importantly, he's issued an ID card giving him full run of the city, enabling him to ignore the curfew and the air-raid sirens. He doesn't yet know it, but of all the pieces of paper he'll ever hold—a wad of banknotes, a passport, his children's birth certificates—this one may be the most precious by far. But there's a downside: Now that my father is in uniform, he can't be seen with his family. They work out rendezvous spots where he can pass off a parcel of food, take a packet of mail to send.

Back in the yellow star house, Muki, Csurka, and Csupi stave off raw despair. Muki sends beseeching letters to his contacts from the bank: Embassy officials, employees of the Swiss Red Cross, anyone who might offer them shelter. His letters are snowflakes crushed beneath an avalanche. Every Jew in the city is doing the same thing, grasping at the iron bars of their cages, desperate for some way out. Chilling rumors are filtering in from the countryside, where Hungary's cities and towns are being emptied of their Jews. Rounded up into makeshift jails—warehouses, disused breweries, livestock pens—they're herded to rail yards where they're stuffed into windowless cattle cars. Where do they go after that? No one seems to know, but one thing is certain: This is what "deportation," the word on everyone's lips, must mean. And whatever it is, it's not good. Now an antidote appears: Doctors are doing a brisk trade in cyanide capsules.

Outside, in his disguise, my father is grateful. As his ambulance picks its way through bombed-out streets, its arrival inspires expressions of naked hope. To my father's surprise, the horrific injuries they encounter don't unsettle him: Limbs crushed beneath a collapsed ceiling, a man screaming as his ear dangles from the side of his face by a thin elastic band of skin. My father toys with the idea of becoming a doctor and, sensing this, one of the LEGO unit's surgeons takes him under his wing. "Injury is nothing more than tissue disarranged by trauma," he tells him, and this simple mantra helps him make sense of the disordered bodies he finds.

Just as I'll become entranced by the nighttime world, now my father finds himself in thrall to the dark. In his uniform he's no longer a Jew hiding from the playground bullies. He's a soldier, or something resembling one, traversing darkened streets lit only by the ambulance's hooded headlights. Overhead, the sky is split by the surreal jags of tracer shells and probing electric searchlights. It is terrifying and eerily beautiful. During the daylight raids the city is like a terrarium, held under a great dome of glass:

> *The planes were so high as to be completely inaudible and, at first, even invisible; only their long white condensation trails, in impeccable formation, would be visible, with occasionally a glint of sunshine on an aluminum fuselage. It was a thrill for me to watch them: Men fighting to defeat the Nazis, and thus to liberate me, and at the same time bringing deathly danger to me and to my city. Every once in a while, a bright orange speck of an explosion, a darker trail of smoke or tiny white parachutes told a different story. My comrades cheered and I swallowed unshed tears.*

American bombers come by day, English and Russian ones by night. Day and night, night and day, the bombing continues, slackening and then intensifying again. Sometimes the sirens sound four or five times a day. *The Jews control the raids through secret signaling devices*, goes the rumor. They're no longer Hungarians, barely even human; why should they be protected from their own bombs? In early June, a decree is read on the radio: *"Jews can use shelters only when the number of Christians wanting to use them is not large,"* says the announcer. *"When there is no place for Jews, they should look for protection in some other way."*

At the LEGO barracks, my father learns the limits of his comrades' forbearance. During his shifts, he sleeps and takes his meals there. But on days off, he quickly finds that his presence draws suspicious glances. Friends and acquaintances allow him the use of an unused bed or a floor to nap on, but even being seen near an unfamiliar apartment is exceedingly dangerous. If the wrong person asks a probing question, the game is up. And these days, it seems, everyone is asking questions. In the first days of the occupation, the Germans are overwhelmed by denunciations: Some 35,000 citizens report their neighbors for the crime of being Jewish. And so my father learns how to become invisible: Sleeping his way through double features; stretching a bowl of soup at a diner to the limit; whiling away long hours walking the streets.

The next month, August, things change again. Romania—Hungary's arch nemesis, bound to it only by their shared alliance with Hitler—surrenders to the Soviets. Suddenly, the war is very close. Admiral Horthy's regime fumbles; the prime minister dismisses his pro-German cabinet members; police hold back a massive fascist demonstration. More rumors: The Americans are going to parachute in, just like in Normandy; Hungary is on the verge of surrender; Hitler wants a word with Horthy.

Horthy has a secret plan. On October 15, 1944—another of those brilliantly sunny Sundays—the country will surrender to the Soviets. Word goes out that an important pronouncement is to be read, and Budapest is electric with expectation. At 1pm Horthy takes to the radio, delivering a long diatribe proclaiming Hungary's innocence. It is cynical, self-serving, and patently false, but at least it's a renunciation of Germany. Celebrations break out: People pour out into the streets, everyone shouting excitedly at once. *Better late than never!* Jews rip off their yellow stars. *We are saved!*

Here's what really happens: Hungary's plan to defect is half-hearted and amateurish. The rollout is bungled, and only a single infantry division switches sides. What's more, the Gestapo have been tracking it all along. A team of German commandos seizes Admiral Horthy's son, threatening to execute him unless the regent cedes power. As Horthy capitulates, Hungary squanders its last chance to save itself.

Now, after his wilderness years, Ferenc Szálasi and the Arrow Cross party are back. There could be no worse choice. Placed in power by the Führer, himself in the throes of paranoia and late-stage opiate dependence, Szálasi is grasping and grandiose, manifestly unequal to the moment. Later, he will be diagnosed a full-fledged schizophrenic. For the time being, he commands an entire country and its army.

The game is over; the schoolyard bullies have been let loose. The Arrow Cross have Adolf Hitler's blessing and they'll no longer settle for pushing soft Jewish boys down in the playground dirt. They carry rifles, grenades, evil-looking German machine guns given them by the SS. They carry them everywhere: in the street, on trams, shopping for groceries. Some are angry-eyed boys no older than my father; others are middle-aged men desperate for one more chance to pull a trigger. They are cartoon villains in armbands, even calling each other "brother," like proper goons. But they are not cartoons. They are ordinary men—and not a few women—driven to murderous rage by all their missed opportunities, the years of watching life pass by as Hungary writhed under the strictures of Trianon and the Depression. Now it's the Jews who will pay for Hungary's defilement.

The rumors sifting in from the countryside are true: There are no Jews left outside the capital. The *gendarmes,* the loathsome military police, have delivered them to the Germans, but not before enacting an orgy of violence and degradation themselves. Now, at last, it's Budapest's turn. The very night of Horthy's abortive surrender attempt, the Arrow Cross begin patrolling the streets. They seize anyone without papers, anyone with papers they deem forgeries, anyone with proper papers who somehow seems Jewish anyway. They march them down to the banks of the Danube, men and women and children now caught in the lunatic gears, each of them making their silent peace or pleading against what is to come. The Danube waits for them, insatiable.

That night, a new sound arises: The chattering of giant teeth. A pause for a fresh belt of ammunition, then the teeth start up again. My father listens from the barracks, where he hides among men who would have fewer qualms about turning him in than killing a rat with a garden spade. All that separates my father from the guns is the paper-thin scrim of his disguise. Surely it is only a matter of time.

As I perch with my laptop on my knees, the thunder echoing off the walls of the courtyard sounds like the booming of distant guns. I've read my father's recollections before, of course. But it's only now, subsumed in the awfulness of what's to come, that I finally have some inkling of the dread he felt writing them.

I am under slept and disoriented. The night before I lay awake for hours, feeling the dread coiling around my wrists and ankles. And yet its nature is changing. Now that I'm actually *doing* something—even if it's only writing my family's story—I feel surer of myself. Just as in ayahuasca, I'm engaging with fears that only recently felt unfeelable; as I do, I feel their grip loosening. I can't stop the tundra from melting, or pretend I've done anything noteworthy. But I am here, at the very site of my family's ordeal, and I'm determined to stop living my life in its shadow. I think of Julianna and Evelyn back home, the trust they've put in me. The crucible of marriage and fatherhood, the therapy and the medicine work, the reconnection with my family: This is what it's all been for. I want to be a better husband, a better father, a better friend, and with this I feel a tender rush of emotion. I fire up the first stovetop espresso of the day, open my notebook, and begin uploading the previous day's audio recordings. It's time to get to work.

48

Budapest, May 2019: I've collected a list of offices and organizations where I might find a paper trail: The military archives, the Jewish genealogy archive behind the Dohanyi Street synagogue. But the closer I get to these storehouses of certitude, the less certain I feel. What could these microfilms and records tell me, anyway? The name of Muki's artillery unit, or the *gymnásia* my grandmother attended? These aren't facts I actually care about; it may not be facts I'm seeking at all. And so I look for the floating cottonwood blossoms instead; they seem to know where I'm headed before I do.

Spring is in full bloom, and the sky alternates between days-long rains and washes of golden glowing light. But the faces around me are not so sunny. As I walk the subway platforms and wait in comically long supermarket checkouts, I search Budapesters' eyes for kindness but it's hard to find. Women's eyes are narrow beneath the brash hair coloring I call "Eastern European Red." Men's faces are pinched and hard, darkened by alcohol and sun. I see only hostile glares, and soon I stop trying to make eye contact. Still, I'm halfway through my trip before I finally admit how grateful I am not to have been born here.

This morning, the cottonwood tufts lead me towards the Castle District. I've become fixated on my father's time in LEGO. There's no mention of the organization in my references and I want confirmation, some proof of my father's shockingly bold act of subterfuge. He wrote that there was once a photograph of him in uniform with Csupi—her purse held in a studied way so as to hide the yellow star stitched to her overcoat—but it's long since disappeared. Just a mental image of him would help cement this crucial moment in the story; lacking a visual reference it feels gauzy and ephemeral.

As I wander around the back of the castle complex, I stumble across a discreet stone-faced portal in the side of the hill: "Sziklakórház: Hospital in the Rock." I've heard of it, but I can't remember where. Interesting, but not on my list of must-see sites. Plus, the entrance fee is steep by Budapest standards. But as I dawdle outside, that feeling comes again: The unseen hand on my chest. As if to underscore the hint, distant thunder booms off the Buda Hills. I walk inside and buy a ticket.

As I sit down inside the dinky theater, a wheezy digital projector plays a short introductory video. Now I understand that ghostly sensation: The hospital was also a LEGO command post. The film cuts to a snatch of wartime newsreel, and I go bolt upright, gape-mouthed. On the screen, an ambulance—military grey, a large red cross on its side, just as my father described—pulls up to the hospital entrance. Out leap two stretcher bearers, each in khaki overalls and....

There is my father.

It isn't, of course. It can't be; the man's height and movements are wrong. But a decades-old memory tumbles forth: I'm sitting in my father's lap and he's telling me about this fantastical hospital, a system of corridors and chambers tunneled into the caves below a castle. He must have come here often: His LEGO unit was sited just down the hill, roughly a mile away. The feeling inside my chest is nearly painful, nervous receptors fully awake as these ancient signals finally reach my antennae. Time is bending back on itself, and I feel as though I'm back in ayahuasca. As much as the sheer chance of my stumbling onto this footage, it's the recognition that follows in its wake that floors me. In addition to their khaki overalls, each stretcher-bearer wears a *stahlhelm*, the iconic German-style helmet. Outside the swastika, it is perhaps the most recognizable symbol of Nazism.

So far as the rest of the world was concerned, my father was a Nazi soldier.

When the film ends, a few minutes later, I'm caught in an in-between realm (the premise for yet another *Star Trek* episode, "Mirror, Mirror"). The air feels charged; anything is possible. My fellow viewers—a half-dozen or so—stand up to begin the guided tour. "Photographs are strictly prohibited," the guide reminds us, but I lag behind to covertly snap as many as I can, as if I might ensnare some echo of my father's presence here.

The hospital is unsettling. Because the complex is carved out of natural caves, the air is dank and still. Offices and surgical theaters appear at unexpected junctures in the arched passageways. In one cubicle I see a display case of vintage medical supplies, including amyl nitrate tablets like the ones Csurka depended upon for her worsening heart pains. In another cavern I'm drawn to a large piece of equipment labeled "Röntgen." I remember that in Europe, X-ray machines are named for the physicist who pioneered their use, though why I know this I can't recall.

The rooms are outfitted with convincing-looking mannequins, many with realistically gory wounds. I'm grateful the curators haven't chosen to depict the final stage of the siege, when the hospital became a horror show. Thanks to a book I brought from Portland—Krisztián Ungváry's *Battle for Budapest*—I know the staff were overwhelmed by an unquenchable flood of wounded soldiers and civilians, many horrifically maimed. After the power and water failed, surgeons worked by lantern as basic medical supplies—clean bandages, antiseptic, anesthesia—ran out. Now another flood began: The sewers backed up, filling the hallways with human waste and cloaking the wounded and dying in their own filth. For many of them, there was only one way out. Later, survivors described the flat crack of pistol shots reverberating through the corridors as medics dispatched the hopeless.

When the tour finally ends and I emerge back into daylight, I gulp the fresh air. Between the claustrophobic tunnels, the grimacing mannequins, and the unexpected encounter with my father, I feel overwhelmed. I pause on a bench outside the War Museum. Pal told me that whenever my father came to Budapest, he'd always visit this place. Now I understand why: It's full of exhibits about the White War, where Muki battled in the mountains over a century ago. My father came to this very spot, again and again, trying to find the quiet and self-contained man who'd raised him. The thought fills me with grief: sons chasing fathers in perpetuity.

For all my father's elusiveness, now it seems like he's everywhere: Captured on the filmstrip, resting beside me on this bench, echoed in the angled loops of my own handwriting. I've crossed half the globe to find him, and now—taunted by the ghosts who flit about me, just out of reach—I know it's myself I must face. I feel like I'm in ayahuasca once again, face to face with my darkest fears.

Right now, they're winning. It's too late to change, and I'm only following the path laid out for me. From Muki's slow-burning anxiety to my father's propensity to vanish, the men in my line have always found ways to hide. I feel something coming undone inside me, a sadness tinged with awe. I've changed so much over the last few years, and yet I've only reached the starting line. For a long span of minutes, I wonder if I have the will to keep going. *Will it always be this hard?*

I rouse myself from my torpor and walk down towards the Danube; twenty minutes later, I'm standing at its bank. As I gaze at the water another story floats back to me, about my father's friend Tommy. He was one of those luckless Jews caught up in the Arrow Cross sweeps and taken here to die. Instead, he was reborn: At the last instant, he turned his head. Rather than severing his spine at the neck—the Arrow Cross's preferred method—the bullet passed through his cheeks. It shattered his jaw, but it didn't kill him. He dropped into the frigid water with the corpses and managed to swim away to a boat-launching stage, where some soldiers pulled him out. Then—this being the most remarkable part, to me at least—rather than finishing him off themselves, they took him to a hospital.

I startle from my reverie. It's a beautiful late-spring afternoon. Happy tourists form eddies around me as I stand transfixed. The tragedy of this place is mine, should I choose to claim it. I could spend the rest of my life plumbing its sorrow, enfolding my-self in its darkness. But I know how that story ends; it's time to write a new one. Frozen in the wonder of this knowing, I stand here a moment longer as the human tide ripples and flows all around me. Then I join it, stepping onto the Chain Bridge and pressing across to the other side.

49

Budapest, May 2019: As I walk along the river I feel borne on a newfound sense of possibility. Something has broken free inside, and I'm in flow once again. My family's story has waited for me all along; all that was required was for me to close my eyes and look for it. Now the Margit Bridge looms before me and, just like that, another of my father's stories floats back to me. It's about the day the bridge blew up, and what happened afterwards.

It was November 4th, 1944. A Saturday. With the Soviets drawing close, a crew of German sappers was sent to mine the bridge in preparation for the coming assault, but somehow no one thought to close it to pedestrian traffic. Whether it was a cigarette thrown by a passer-by or a spark from one of the Danube's long-funneled tugboats passing underneath, in an instant a titanic explosion obliterated the eastern span of the bridge. As many as six hundred people were killed: Pedestrians, truck drivers, an entire passenger tram, all blown sky-high or plunged into the icy river below. My father remembered the moment well. He'd crossed the bridge himself only minutes before, and was startled out of his wits by the explosion behind him.

Now that the bridge was gone, my father had to take a ferry to get from Pest to the LEGO barracks in Buda. The way he told it, one chilly morning he stepped on board to find a stomach-churning sight: A Gestapo officer with a squad of troops. They had a prisoner with them and, what's more, my father knew him: A guy from his old neighborhood. With a barely perceptible nod, my father acknowledged him and turned away. But his nod was not imperceptible; the German officer saw it and arrested him on the spot. Once the ferry reached the Buda side, he was taken to the police station on Margit Boulevard.

My father was led downstairs to a large holding cell. Inside were a handful of other prisoners and a single, bored-looking guard, a German sub-machine gun dangling from his shoulder. My father was close to panic. Convinced there was no way he would escape with his life, a desperate thought began to take hold. What if he wrestled the gun away from the guard and shot his way out? He surely wouldn't make it out the front door, but if he took down even a single German officer on the way, wouldn't that be enough?

Weighing the chances of his suicide dash, my father began to choreograph his make-or-break tussle with the guard. As his eyes slid down the gun, his stomach lurched again: It wasn't a German gun, but a Hungarian copy. This changed everything. Was there a thumb latch or an extra safety? He knew he couldn't overpower the guard through sheer strength. If he wasted precious seconds fumbling to charge the gun, his heroic dash was going to look more like the death spasms of the chickens he'd seen the cook at his uncle's country estate kill: Headless, shambling, and spurting a trail of thick blood. My father plunged deeper and deeper into despair.

An hour went by, then two. But then: A miracle! An officer appeared at the cell gate with his papers. My father was released.

I've only heard the story once, which already makes me suspect it. But it's too gripping to discard completely: My father in mortal danger, even contemplating murder. Could it be too good to be true? I scan back in memory, recalling the sound of my father's voice. Do I detect a strange tension? Is it the strain of recalling the danger he'd faced, or the knowledge that some details—*or maybe all of them*—were carefully burnished?

I even researched the gun in question: The MP40, the iconic German sub-machine gun, a sleek, evil-looking piece of machinery. But Hungary never produced its own copy. In fact, only the week before, Stacey and I walked past a shop selling air-powered sport guns. Spotting a replica MP40 on the wall, I asked the clerk if there was a Hungarian version. A swarthy and terrifyingly built man covered in tattoos, he laughed and said no, though his expression suggested he'd happily stick the muzzle up my ass, just for kicks.

But then, a couple of days later, YouTube's predictive algorithm offered an alternate explanation: a video about Hungary's native gun, the Kiraly 43M. The Hungarians didn't copy the German gun, but made one of their own. Did it look like the German gun? That depends on your perspective. They were both sub-machine guns, with obvious similarities and obvious differences. It didn't settle the matter, but still: The question was less black-or-white than I'd supposed. I was starting to see Stacey's point: Why did it seem so important to prove whether or not our father had lied?

By the time I reach my cousin's flat and unlock the heavy gate, the story has become a Möbius strip, an intractable loop toggling between *True* and *False*. Resigning myself to another night of broken sleep, I eat a simple dinner and lie down. Pal is away with his girlfriend this week, but tomorrow I'll see his father, Antal. Perhaps he can shed some light on my father's tales.

50

Budapest, May 2019: The next morning I wake up bright and early, excited for this reunion. On the walk to the tram I stop at the fanciest of the patisseries off Jászai Mari Square to purchase treats for us: Slices of *Dobos* torte—an archeological dig of spongecake, chocolate buttercream, and caramel—and dense slabs of Black Forest cake for good measure.

Twenty minutes later I'm standing before the entrance of a discreetly elegant apartment building in Buda. As I reach the third-floor landing, I stop in amazement. Deborah was right: Waiting there for me is my father's double. For a long moment I'm speechless, and Antal laughs quietly, fully aware of the resemblance. We embrace, and then he leads me inside the flat he shares with his wife, Aliz. They laugh again as I present my package from the bakeshop. Naturally, they've procured delicacies as well: Chocolate-dipped macaroons, jam-filled *kolachy*, dense brown-sugar shortbread. We agree that we're well-provisioned enough to get us through the afternoon.

The flat is a tidier, more elegant version of Pal's. The walls are covered in 20th-century art: Stark etchings, moody oil paintings, dramatic sketches in black ink. I'm startled to recognize a pair of nature studies: The artist was a distant relative, and I grew up under a pair of his evocative watercolors. Finally, we sit down at the antique dining table to talk. Antal's English is halting, Aliz's not a great deal better. But I'm practically vibrating with excitement. They depart for Germany the next morning, so this will be my only opportunity to see them. With this deadline looming, the conversation quickly deepens.

It's not just Antal's appearance that's familiar. As he switches between Hungarian and English, his cadence—even the way he clears his throat—all remind me of my father. I'm moved by this auditory time capsule, and I'm boggled by what I'm learning. Antal and I share common grandparents in Muki and Csurka, but his memories of them are utterly foreign to me. As he haltingly unreels his recollections, I feel once again as though I'm seeing the dark side of our family's moon.

When Antal was born, just after the war, Budapest was a ruined city, burnt out and starving. Food, electricity and running water were tenuous; the family depended upon food drops from the U.S. Army Air Corps. I'm reminded of one of my father's strange rituals. Every now and again, the man who'd seen the inside of most of France's Michelin-starred restaurants would crack open, of all things, a can of Spam. "For me," he'd quietly intone, "it is the taste of freedom."

Antal was fortunate not to be one of the countless orphans growing up in Europe's ashes, though he might as well have been. His mother, my Aunt Csupi, was self-absorbed and unreliable. His father, Andor—the one who'd arranged my father's forged birth certificate—was already descending into schizophrenia, eyes often so distant they looked dead. So Antal was raised by Muki and Csurka instead. As I listen in rapt attention, he describes a childhood from an alternate reality.

After the 1949 Socialist takeover, my grandparents were relocated to a communal flat with a complete stranger, an erratic and muttering older woman named Elza. She'd returned from a concentration camp a hollow shell of herself. Outside, it was worse. It was the height of Stalinism, a state of more or less constant paranoia. "The first foreign words I learned was '*Nicht für Kinder*,'" says Antal. I know the phrase too, though I don't speak German: *Not for children.* "Yes, my ears would grow double when

I heard the adults say that! Like when the neighbor was taken away in the night. He was beaten so hard he couldn't even walk."

Csurka and Antal were close, and she often took him on errands. His favorite stop was near the ruins of the Margit Bridge, where a fisherman lived on a small boat. "Yes," says Antal. "That's where she'd buy a fish for...."

"*Rácz-ponty!*" I finish for him. Like a talisman, my grandmother's Serbian-style carp dish recurs over and over through the decades. Antal smiles warmly. "Yes, I tried to make it too, but it didn't taste even half of hers!"

With this, the conversation veers towards the happier memories of foods. And it's now that a strange thing happens. I mention my last visit here with my father, and the vegetable soup Aliz made from her kitchen garden. "Ah, yes," she remembers. "Your father loved a sour herb called *sóska*; I would always save some for him."

That gentle hand on my chest again. *Sour herb? Does she mean sorrel?* She thinks for a moment. "Yes! That's the one. I would make his favorite dish: Boiled beef with sorrel sauce."

Now another of those trapdoors swings wide inside me. That was the same dish I'd ordered at random at the old-fashioned diner a few weeks before. As I ate it, I'd heard someone in the background intoning my father's long-lost nickname: *Gyuri*. My father's favorite dish? Until then I'd never even heard of it.

My skin feels flushed. "Tell me more about his visits here," I ask. "Pal told me that my father would help out with household chores here, like clearing brush or painting a room." What I left unsaid was that back home, he'd never have performed those tasks himself; he'd simply order me to do them instead.

"Yes, it was very strange. Here he was a famous international lawyer, busy all the time, but every trip he would spend a day like this, with us."

I wonder aloud what other activities he undertook here. Stacey and I have often speculated that our father entertained girlfriends here, and Antal surely must know that the marriage to Irene was less than harmonious. Antal and Aliz exchange a look. She rises to fetch a small photo album. Inside are photos of a backyard dinner party; it looks like the late '80s or early '90s. Gathered around a wooden table set with bottles of white wine are Antal and Aliz, a couple of my father's Hungarian friends, and an older woman. Her grey hair is cut in a trim wave, her expression frank but not unkind. "She was almost like his girlfriend," says Aliz.

I'm stunned. I've never seen or heard of this woman before. I grin and look Antal directly in the eye. "*Like* his girlfriend?"

"His girlfriend."

Who had he really been? I marveled at the intricacies of my father's alternate life. Here he could be the one who'd escaped and made good: Staying in the fanciest hotels, treating everyone to drinks and meals. So what if his marriages were icebound and his children alienated? I'm drifting deeper into introspection when another of those conversational lurches jolts me out of my reverie. Antal is recounting a story from the last year of the war, when my father was in his LEGO disguise. Because of the language barrier, it takes me a moment to understand what he's saying. But when I do, I'm at full attention. Without my having prompted him, he's telling the story of my father's arrest.

"…His friend saw him in the military blouse, how do you say it?" says Antal.

"His LEGO uniform! Yes yes yes, okay," I blurt out. "George only told me this story once. He never repeated it, and so I didn't know if it was true." My heart is in my throat, but I press on as evenly as I can.

"So, let me get this straight. Someone sees him in uniform acknowledging his Jewish friend and says 'Why are you talking to a Jew?' Who takes him? The Germans? Or the *Nyilas*, the Arrow Cross?"

"No, the *Nyilas*," Antal nods. "They look at his papers, they say 'It is not enough.' So they bring him to a Röntgen."

I'm dumbfounded. Does he really mean an X-ray machine, the same kind I saw the day before in the Hospital in the Rock? I instantly see what he's getting at. Just as the Nazis were obsessed with cranial geometry as an indicator of racial purity, the Arrow Cross believed in a master "Turanian-Hungarian" race, even resorting to collecting skull measurements with calipers. But there's no evidence they ever resorted to X-raying their captives. In fact, many who survived this time remember a far more expedient method, one which every Jewish male came to fear above all others. Just as my father was shoved into the playground dirt, his pants pulled down by the bullies, now the men of the Arrow Cross took to examining their male captives' genitals, right there on the street. Failing the test was an immediate death sentence.

"But…that doesn't make any sense," I say. "There are easier ways to check."

Antal's expression is neutral. "Did he tell you this? You should ask Csupi, it is her story."

Now Aliz pipes in: "Do you know George was in Korean War?" I can hardly believe my ears. It was my offhand remark about Korea—years ago, in that chance encounter with my father's first wife, Ruth—that cracked open this entire quest.

"He wasn't," I say gently.

"*Nem?* No?" says Antal.

"No. I requested his military records after he died."

"George's family didn't know this," says Aliz. Like Antal, her tone is neutral, not accusatory. I'm grateful. More than anyone else, it's them I want to protect from the notion that my father lied. But the mood is strangely calm; it feels as though we're held inside a gentle spell. I trust that they know I'm not here to settle old scores, and with this comes the sense of an eggshell gently beginning to crack.

I'm starting to see my father's stories on a deeper level. At dinner a few weeks before, Stacey had conjured the world of *Tintin*, the Belgian comics I loved reading with my father. Now I wonder if his stories are both Tintinesque projections and a dissociation from a nightmarish reality. In these movie-memories he could command a tank in Korea, or blithely contemplate machine-gunning Gestapo officers.

The afternoon light is waning, and Antal and Aliz have to prepare for tomorrow morning's trip. I take my leave, my ruck-sack bulging with leftover cookies. Antal has survived so much more than I ever will; now his solidity and groundedness give me heart. In the fading light I walk most of the way back to Pal's apartment, stopping to buy a few flaccid vegetables from a gloomy basement supermarket.

Today's conversation has shaken the snow globe. At last I have corroboration for a few of my father's stories, but still no proof. All the answers lead only to more questions. I'm starting to grasp that, like me, my father wasn't two people—one of them truthful, the other dishonest—but a single person altered by trauma. But he'd never done the work of reuniting the splintered parts of himself. Had he even tried? I see now, with a twinge of sadness, that it was more important for my father to be admired than for him to be known.

I accept, finally, that it's time to call Aunt Csupi.

51

Budapest, May 2019: The next morning I awaken as bleary and unrested as ever. As I stretch and gaze out over the city, echoes of yesterday's conversation ricochet inside me. When Antal was describing his early life under Socialism, he'd mentioned my own trauma: Rhonda's death. So had Poki during our first dinner together. Each time they did the barometer seemed to dip. I knew they both loved me, but the suspicion that they saw me as fundamentally damaged felt exquisitely uncomfortable. *Of course he couldn't have made something of himself.*

But in dawn's gentle light I see the untruth of these internal tape loops. If Rhonda had lived, maybe I'd be running a thriving medical practice or traveling around Europe enjoying my well-earned retirement. But this is simply the shape my life has taken, and in the last few years that shape has changed, radically. I'm no longer in free fall; I can feel the web of handholds and supports I've built for myself. I feel more present and awake than I ever have, and I'm learning the truth of where I came from and who I really am. For today at least, that's enough. I open my laptop and plug in my ear buds. Taking a deep breath, I click the button and Skype Csupi.

"Hallo?" Her voice sounds frailer than I remembered it. She recognizes mine immediately, which pleases me. Then again, I suspect she doesn't get many calls; if I need a reminder as to why, it's not long in coming.

"Seth! How wonderful that you called!" she purrs. "I am in a nursing home. It is very hard, the Swiss are very enemylike."

Enemylike? "But Csupi," I say brightly, "your health is remarkable for a woman of your age!"

"Yes, well. There is one doctor here, but he is very stupid and he hates me."

"Um, that's unfortunate." After a few minutes more of chitchat—it's never difficult to deflect questions about my life back to her own—I cautiously unveil my line of interrogation for the day.

"So, Csupi. Tell me about when you had to leave Szász Károly Street. Is that when you went to Falk Miksa Street?"

If hearing that name is a shock, it doesn't register. I often find that when it pleases her, Csupi can toggle between the decades with ease. Now is one of those moments: With only the gentlest of nudges, I've swung open the heavy door to a vault. As she drops back into the summer of 1944 I type notes in double time, trying to keep up with the memories pouring forth.

"I don't like to remember Falk Miksa *utca*," she says, using the Hungarian. "This was the first place we fled to. A 'yellow star' house, the entrance was painted with a big star." Her voice is even and clear, though it must be decades since she's told anyone this. "It was a very humiliating time. Just an atmosphere of constant fear; so many things happened every day. When the Germans came, we knew we were through. They were so *thorough*, we knew they would finish us."

As she speaks and I take frantic dictation, films unspool behind my eyes. I know that at first, the yellow star houses offered Budapest's Jews a modicum of protection. Later, after Admiral Horthy's failed surrender attempt, they became something else: A place for the Arrow Cross to sharpen their teeth, to find out what it felt like to force open a door, to seize a stranger and put a pistol to his head. Right there in the hallway, in front of his pleading wife and children, taking their watches and jewelry from shaking hands, then pulling the trigger anyway, leaving him to spill out onto the elegant tiled floors.

I snap out of my reverie. "Not everyone supported the Germans," says Csupi. "People we didn't even know would come to help us. A young woman, what was her name? Emmi… Emmi Haessler, yes, she would visit and bring food. I gave her some money after the war. She brought us coats and dresses from Szász Károly."

After a pause, she continues. "A man came one evening, a friend of a girlfriend. I hardly knew her, but she'd paid the man to hide me. He took me to his apartment and gave me some food.

But when I went to the little bed he'd prepared, he just sat there and stared at me." Heart in my throat, I wait for her to continue.

"Then Muki was taken away for a few days," she continues, leaving the story hanging. "After he came back, he never spoke about it again." At this another jigsaw piece snaps satisfyingly into place. My father once told me that through Muki's international connections at the bank, he'd convinced his captors to free him, though I don't know any more details than Csupi does.

With the Arrow Cross in power it was clear that staying in the yellow star house could only mean death. But where could they go? At last, a bolt of pure luck: "Ella Barrey brought us to a Red Cross house," says Csupi, and with this another puzzle piece finds its home. Ella Barrey was my grandmother's best friend. By an incredible stroke of good fortune, she worked at the International Committee of the Red Cross. In the last months of the war, the organization mobilized to save Budapest's Jews, renting dozens of apartments and placing official notices of protection outside them. With Csupi running from hideout to hideout and Muki having already been arrested once, Ella arranged for the family to move to a Red Cross house. It was no guarantee, but it was better than nothing.

"I contacted Ella and she took me in as an employee," says Csupi. "I could write shorthand and knew the languages. I wrote down people's data, sleeping two hours a night. Only once came the police, someone warned us. They hid me somewhere, down in the cellar. I spent maybe half a day there. I don't remember; I don't want to."

I push ahead: "Csupi, where was my father during this time? Was he already with the LEGO?"

"Yes, yes, that's where George found a job. He had papers and could go out; he would pick up people in an ambulance. But he was always gone to clean up after the raids."

"So," I offer as casually as I can, "did he ever tell you about his arrest? After the Margit Bridge blew up?"

"Well, I saw him being taken away."

My heart skips a beat. "What…what do you mean?" I ask, as coolly as I can manage.

"I saw him being taken to the police station on Margit Boulevard. I went back to Muki and Csurka white as a ghost, but I couldn't tell them what had happened. When he came back, many hours later, I almost fainted."

I am learning, almost, to anticipate these twists. But now I am silent for a long moment, unsure of what to believe or even to think.

"That was just before the Red Cross house. And you know that Muki was taken away again and that George saved him, right?"

I do know this story, though it's been years since I've thought about it. Of all the wisps of memory that have risen up only to evaporate, this one is different. When I was young, it was the origin story that told me who my father was, what I was supposed to live up to. Now, as Csupi's words unleash this memory, it rushes forwards to envelop me completely.

52

Budapest, November 1944: The end of 1944 is bitterly cold, the start of a winter so brutal it's as if the Earth itself has had enough of this war. A new species of bird appears in the skies above Budapest. Red Air Force *shturmoviks*: ugly, purposeful-looking things with red stars painted on their flanks. They swarm overhead, raking anything that moves with machine-cannons, smashing the city building by building and body by body with cluster bombs.

Now the occupants of the yellow star houses are herded to the ghetto in the center of Pest, where some 70,000 souls are forced into an area encompassing a tenth of a square mile. The streets run with sewage and human waste. Men and women curl into fetal positions, many suffering from typhus: covered in bleeding rashes, wracked by diarrhea and cramps. Children roam amongst the corpses stacked to the ceilings of shuttered cafés, left on street corners or lying on the frozen ground. The little park in Klauzál Square, where seventy-five years hence I'll take my meals in leisure, is a mass grave. Each day, the Arrow Cross break in to seize more victims. The sound of gunfire coming from the river is ceaseless.

And now Muki has been taken. The Labor Service still demands Jewish bodies and, just as my father was called up when the age limits were relaxed, now *his* father has been summoned as well. At first, the laborers are put to work around Budapest, where they're reasonably safe. But the Germans, determined to wring every last drop of blood from their erstwhile ally, order tens of thousands to walk west through freezing rain and snow towards Austria. The men—lacking food, shelter, or adequate clothing—are on a literal death march. Nobody knows how many die, beaten or shot by their Arrow Cross guards or simply left by the road. A realization gnaws at my father: If Muki leaves Budapest, he will never be seen again.

It's time to pull some strings. At the Red Cross, Csupi manages to wrangle an official-looking order for Muki's release. With his precious LEGO identification my father can roam the city at will, but he needs a vehicle and someone to drive it. And while it risks revealing everything—his true identity, his mother and sister's precarious hiding place—my father bribes the most sympathetic-seeming LEGO crewman. The next day, in a borrowed ambulance, they set out looking for Muki.

My father knows that Jewish laborers are being held on the outskirts of town, in warehouses and other industrial sites. But where? Budapest is not a small city. The brick factory in Óbuda is full to bursting with miserable detainees, but no Muki. The barracks at Kelenföld? Nothing. Slaughterhouses, quarries, everywhere he sees yellow-starred men under guard, they stop. No Muki.

The driver grows more anxious by the hour. The giant red crosses aside, a vehicle in military grey is a perfect target for the terror birds wafting above. The driver steers with his neck craned painfully upwards. When he spots a *shturmovik,* he careens off the road until it drones away.

Outside is a vision from hell. The ambulance passes lines of emaciated men, women, and children in yellow stars digging anti-tank ditches. Columns of bedraggled Hungarian and German soldiers—old men and teenaged boys, just like my father—stream back from the front, now just miles away. Miserable Hungarian Jews and Russian POWs in rags shuffle westward towards their anonymous deaths. As they pass them by, my father scans every face in near-panic. No Muki.

The sun is leaving the sky. The driver, openly hostile now, delivers an ultimatum: One more stop and then he will turn the ambulance around, with or without my father's precious cargo. Desperate, and with only a few minutes remaining till nightfall, my father spots a brewery in Kőbánya, an industrial suburb near the airport. He asks the driver to pull over. Inside the warehouse is a scene of utter despair: Gaunt, downcast men in yellow stars huddling in the frigid damp, surrounded by piles of garbage and filth. My father scans the darkening room. Sitting by himself, wrapped in a blanket and visibly ill, is Muki.

For an instant they lock eyes. Neither gives the slightest hint of recognition. Drawing himself up to his full 5' 6", my father strides up to the officer overseeing the captives, a reserve lieutenant, greying and overage. My father clicks his heels and delivers a smart and forceful salute. The lieutenant offers a lazy gesture in return. My father holds out the Red Cross order, his hand barely stilled from shaking. In the most officious tone he can manage, he says: "Lieutenant, I have orders to escort the *Jew...*"—here giving the word what he hopes is a convincing sneer—"...Eugene Lorinczi to the Red Cross office in Pest!"

My young father's heart is running off its rails.

Later, he can't remember if the lieutenant even looks at the document. He certainly doesn't read it. For a long moment he only looks at my father. If anything strikes him as odd—why this soft-faced boy has Red Cross papers for an anonymous Jewish slave—he says nothing.

For a single, interminable moment, the world holds its breath.

Finally, the lieutenant speaks. "Take the bastard," he says, with no more force than a man swatting a gnat from his beer. "I don't care what you do with him."

My father salutes, turns smartly, and strides over to Muki, hauling him to his feet as forcefully as he can manage. Muki, half-starved and weak, can barely walk. The twenty steps back to the ambulance are the longest my father will ever take. My father bundles Muki into a stretcher and slams the back doors. The driver starts the engine and they head back towards Budapest.

It is far easier to head towards the front lines than away from them. It isn't the prowling *shturmoviks* they must fear now, but the checkpoints manned by hard-eyed German military police, just itching to unholster their pistols. Now inspiration strikes: My father covers Muki with a grey army blanket. The police assume they're transporting a corpse, and they nearly are. But it works. Finally, at the close of the most harrowing day of my father's life, the ambulance pulls up to the Red Cross house. "The reunion with Mom and Csupi," my father wrote, "is not within my power to describe."

The story unreels inside me within a fraction of a second. Csupi is still with me, on the other end of the line. I'm awash in brackish water, the past and the present pooling all around me. My father told the story once, when I was maybe ten years old. It's only now I see how it's undergirded my entire life. *This is what a son does for his father.*

How could I possibly match *that?*

I collect myself. It's time, finally, to go out and find what I came here for. "Csupi, what was the street where you sheltered at the end, after George brought Muki back to you? Where the villa was."

"Oh, I can't remember. It was so long ago."

I'm crushed. This whole time, finding the villa has felt absolutely mandatory. For a long moment, I feel as though this whole trip has been a waste. Then Csupi breaks in again. "No! I know…it was 'Penny' street!"

Penny? There are no such names here. Then my boyhood coin collection flashes before my eyes. What's "penny" in Hungarian? *Pengo? Forint?*

"Fillér!" says Csupi triumphantly. "But I don't remember the address. A very beautiful house, at the top of the hill."

She's still talking but I only half-hear her, my fingers racing over the keyboard as I search for *Fillér utca.* It's only later that I'll revisit my notes and understand what it is she's trying to tell me. *There it is! Not twenty minutes away by streetcar.* "Csupi!" I practically shout. "Thank you so much; I love you!" I grab my rucksack and race downstairs to catch the next tram.

53

Budapest, May 2019: Minutes later I'm standing at the base of Fillér Street, a narrow lane winding upwards along the flank of Rose Hill. At its terminus stands one of those round news posts like a stupa. I've walked right by this intersection several times already, never realizing its import. Nerves aquiver, I collect myself and begin walking uphill. After a few minutes a gaseous city bus trundles by, but I'm determined to comb every inch of this road and find the spot where the story ends.

I soon regret this. The road is only a mile long, but it's far steeper than I thought. My rucksack is heavy, the afternoon sun hot. The conversation with Csupi has shaken something loose in me. I can hardly believe what's transpired on this trip thus far, and yet this moment is truly what I came for. I've imagined this place for over forty years, never dreaming I might actually find it. As I trudge uphill, past and present dance round each other like droplets of mercury.

Now it's the end of 1944, and in the bitter cold, food has become scarce. As Budapest swells to absorb untold thousands of refugees, the city becomes a scene of Brueghelian misery. Formations of Red Air Force aircraft patrol the skies, peeling off now and then to bomb a checkpoint or strafe old women waiting for bread. My father struggles to take it all in:

> *The days grew more and more chaotic. The city became overrun with refugees from the advancing Soviet army, the remnants of smashed German and Hungarian army units, prisoners of war under guard, Arrow Cross bands from the parts of the country already overrun by the Soviets, pathetic groups of Jews being herded towards Germany and death camps, Russians in horse-drawn wagons having thrown in their lot with the retreating Germans I suppose, downed British and American fliers, but most of all refugees: Country people with their few animals and possessions, hungry, cold, with crying children, fleeing the terrifying sights and sounds of war.*

My father's LEGO unit is ordered to leave the city and head west, towards Germany. After much soul searching, my father decides to stay in Budapest, stealing off with his uniform and ID card. Being a deserter brings an extra layer of risk, but at least the family is all together, placed in the Red Cross house by Ella Barrey. The owners, wealthy fascists, have fled to Germany. A Red Cross flag flies from a flagpole, an official-looking order of protection framed by the gate. They pray it will be enough.

Perhaps a dozen others—like my family, all of them Jews with lucky connections—have been assigned here, a family to a room. The house is unheated and soon the water will be shut off. Each morning, another piece of furniture is broken up and burned against the cold.

There are tiny mercies, too. The shelves are well-stocked with books, the walls hung with attractive paintings. The final truck convoy from Switzerland has brought tinned vegetables and meat and, somehow, an inexhaustible supply of macaroni. Csurka becomes the house cook, managing to conjure up varied meals from the same staples day after day. If one can just tune out what's happening outside, they might forget they're in a well-appointed prison. All told my family will spend two months hiding here, praying for the war to end.

As I walk up Fillér Street I study each house closely. Some are stately old mansions; others are newer Deco homes. I search for signs of what transpired here, evidence of the violence wrought by the bullets and shell fragments in their thousands, but I see no clues. *A beautiful house at the top of the street*, said Csupi. I keep walking.

Each evening as the city winds down before the air raids, my family hear a strange sound. Not so much a sound as a sensation: a trembling seeming to come from inside the windowpanes. The glass is resonating to the faraway detonations of artillery shells. Csupi recoils from this unnerving sound, or not-sound. *It is the sound of death*, she says. *No*, says my father. *For us, it is the sound of life itself.* My father is fifteen, his sister nineteen. The approach of the Soviets has very different implications for each of them.

At night, during the air raids, everyone gathers in the cellar, where casement windows look out onto the backyard. One night Muki, quiet and aloof as ever, sits apart from the others on the wooden staircase. Blown by a chance gust or released too early by a disoriented bombardier, a stray bomb drifts down and detonates with an ear-shattering crash. A jagged piece of shrapnel smacks through the window like it was made of tissue paper, embedding itself in my grandfather's left temple. Shouts, screams, blood everywhere. My father and another of the residents stagger with Muki to a nearby school, where a makeshift surgical theater has been set up in the basement. There are barely any medical supplies; nurses are boiling pots of melted snow. A surgeon removes the piece of metal by lamplight.

Except for my father in his uniform, none of them leave the house anymore. Bands of Arrow Cross men roam the streets, some of them no longer bothering to check papers at all, instead throwing their captives against a nearby wall for an impromptu execution. The world is ending, the hounds of the Red Army unleashed and bounding closer by the day, and all these men can think to do is snuff out a few more Jewish lives.

The Arrow Cross are kept at bay, mostly, by the official-looking Red Cross order hanging by the gate. Garlic for the vampires. But one day they storm in anyway, a red-faced and panting gang. There is no arguing with them, these simple and terrifying men. They all carry new guns, itching to use them. It is Muki—no papers, a face one would recognize as Jewish from a block away—who is in the gravest danger. He reaches the attic crawlspace in the nick of time. Stuffed just beneath the roof with his face pressed against the joists, he lies frozen in terror. A single cough, a sneeze, a subtle creak of the rafters, anything could tip off the men tramping through the house below. The Arrow Cross are thorough, searching every room, even the one just beneath Muki's trembling body. But missing the discreet trapdoor, they leave. That night Muki, terrified, refuses to go down to the cellar. He will pass the next three weeks stuffed into the crawlspace instead.

The Red Army is already in Pest, smashing the city block by block. The Soviet troops' wooden ammunition crates are stenciled with a directive: *Ne èkonom'te.* It means *"Do not economize,"* and they do not. When they are finished, entire city blocks look as though a giant hurled a hammer down onto them: Bricks, timber, broken glass, the intermingled bodies of what were once horses and people splayed over the majestic boulevards. Later, many survivors will recall the curious beauty of this time, the tracers fracturing the darkness, streaming red and green arcs across the frozen Danube. Star shells—astonishingly bright parachute flares—searing the night sky, bathing the streets in unearthly white.

Winded, I pause to lean on the ancient stone wall that hugs the narrow lane. Did my father once rest here too? As I look towards the city below, another of his stories drifts back to me. One day, at this very spot or one close by, he looks up to see three-engined Junkers Ju 52s, the archaic German transports, dropping supplies to the soldiers below. One of the cylinders drops faster than the others; its parachute has failed to deploy. My father watches in wonder as it drops, ever faster and closer, finally striking the roof of a carriage house down the hill. As if touched by a magic wand, the entire roof turns crimson. After the shock wears off, my father realizes the cylinder must have been filled with bottles of blood.

My father's uniform allows him to leave for brief periods, but it doesn't protect him from danger. One day, near the end, he trudges through meter-thick snow to collect kindling. He watches idly as a *shturmovik* flying only a few hundred feet up drones by before circling lazily back. Fascinated, my father does not drop his kindling or run. He is entranced by the sight of a warplane so close, cannot imagine what business the Red Air Force would have with him, a fifteen-year-old boy—a Jewish one no less—who every night prays the Russians will hasten to save his family. He's forgotten he's wearing a uniform.

The *shturmovik* has drawn a bead on him. My father stares transfixed as the ungainly bird races towards him, rocketing low over the ground at two hundred miles an hour and then passing slightly to one side. Everything else drops away. The sound of the airplane's twelve-cylinder engine is a deafening roar, but my father doesn't hear it. He doesn't hear the clattering of the observer's machine gun, or notice the flashes issuing from the muzzle like fiery belches. Later, all he'll remember is the puzzling sense that the ground is being rent by a titanic sewing machine, a line of stitches throwing up tufts of snow as it races towards him and then runs past only a few feet away.

As the *shturmovik* drones away, the gunner swivels the heavy machine gun back to the centerline. Now my father sees a flash of beautiful auburn hair streaming from underneath her flying helmet. Beneath his feet, bullets hiss quietly in the snow.

54

Budapest, February 1945: No one stands near the windows anymore. Deprived of vision, the war is made of vibration instead. The deathly trembling of the glass has vanished, replaced by an unforgettable buzz: Long, angry swatches like bolts of cloth ripped in two. It's the German machine guns, the MG42s, firing twenty bullets a second; a terrifying buzzsaw blur. The Germans call the gun *knochensäge*—"bone saw"—for what it does to the human body. The crude Soviet sub-machine guns have their own timbre, a *WHAP* like a deck of cards riffling through a giant's hands. Windows, doors, humans simply evaporate into mist before them. Each day the sound gets louder and closer.

When will the Soviets come? Muki is absent, hiding in the attic all the time now. Csurka, the uncomplainer, suffers her chest pains in stoic silence.

Down the hill, in the Castle District, the fetid corridors of the Hospital in the Rock are filled with the wounded and the dying, groaning or suffering in silence. Above their heads the Germans—some 28,000 of them—have been forced onto the hilltop, the same one on which I sat outside the War Museum. This is how the *Wehrmacht* fights, their *Führer* demanding utter loyalty, forbidding retreat until it's far too late. Each day, on average, over ten thousand of his soldiers die. For Adolf Hitler, it is merely another day he lives.

Everyone knows the Germans will stage a breakout; the only question is when. Even now stragglers and deserters creep by the house, hoping to stumble their way to the relief force waiting to the west, or clinging to the slim hope they might simply disappear into the frozen woods until the war is over. Every couple of days, one or two let themselves into the Red Cross house. They stand awkwardly around, the defeated boy soldiers of the Third Reich; some of them Hitler Youth, as young as sixteen. Face to face with their bogeymen, the Jews, the boys seem miserable and afraid. Csupi speaks easily with them in fluent German. "They were so young," she told me. "We only hoped they would not stay, and I was glad when they left. But I was not afraid of them. I hope they died."

I've reached the top of Fillér Street. Scanning the peaked roofs, I see a house that seems right—the cellar encased in stone, the upper floors in weathered stucco—but I can't be sure. I stand outside for long minutes, my aunt's words ringing in my ears. Her native cattiness aside, it's jarring to hear she wished a violent death upon little boys, and that she probably got her wish.

I've brought *Battle for Budapest* in my rucksack. Now I open it and flip to a page that references the very spot where I'm standing. On February 11, 1945, the city long since encircled, *SS Obergruppenführer* Karl Pfeffer-Wildenbruch, the German commander, finally decides to take matters into his own hands, ordering the tens of thousands of German troops in the Castle District to break out. Along with them are untold thousands of panicked civilians.

The house on Fillér Street is directly in their path.

That night, shrouded by a thick blanket of fog, a flood of humanity erupts from the narrow streets of the Castle District like meat from a sausage grinder. The Soviets waiting for them do not even need to aim. As flashes of fire erupt from three sides, the mass of humans becomes a single animal, shoving, kicking, and clawing its way across the killing zone.

I've seen photos of what happened next: The broad plaza of Szena Square, where one day I'll sip espresso and nibble flaky pastries, will be covered by a coarse layer of flesh, pieces of soldiers, civilians, horses all intermingled like scraps on a butcher shop floor. Of the tens of thousands of German soldiers who attempt the breakout, fewer than eight hundred will escape. No one knows how many Hungarian civilians die alongside them.

The soldiers who aren't cut down in the square press up Fillér Street and the nearby lanes, struggling through deep snow. The Soviets are dug in and waiting for them. The sound is deafening, a hail of bullets and shells pouring into the road, cutting down everything before it.

In the cellar, everyone starts as a floor-shaking *THUD* comes from above, sending plumes of dust down on their heads. Upstairs, a wall disintegrates. Someone screams. My father, crouching beneath the cellar windows, hears the growl of a tank nearby, a moment later the titanic *CLANG* of a projectile striking its flank. The shooting is endless, a roar so thick it seems to have physical mass, filling the cellar like floodwater. *There is no way we can survive this.*

The shooting blasts on, ebbing and then roaring back to life. No one sleeps. After an eternity, daylight comes to bathe the stone walls in frigid light. The cellar is deathly cold. The battle has moved on, and it's quieter outside. But occasional bursts of fire—the whapping blur of sub-machine guns, the cracks of rifles—can still be heard, some quite close. Csurka, weary, fetches a pair of buckets and trudges out to collect snow. *What can one do? We must eat.*

Now a new sound comes from upstairs, directly above their heads: The thumping of heavy boots. The Soviets have finally arrived.

55

Budapest, February 1945: The Russians tramp downstairs, sub-machine guns trained on my family. Broad peasant faces stare out from under dun-colored caps, breath steaming in the cold air. A lieutenant is with them. His eyes pass warily over Csurka and Csupi. Gesturing to my father, he says the words every Budapester will come to dread: *Málenkij rabota*. It means "We have a little job for you," but really, it could mean anything.

The soldiers stare at my father. The officer gestures again. With a backwards glance at his family, my father follows the soldiers upstairs. Outside, he finds a party of men: frightened Hungarians, some with Red Army jackets over their civilian clothes. A soldier hands one to my father. It's already been used: There's a fresh bullet hole in the back. The Russians march the men over the crest of Fillér Street and down towards the west where the sounds of fighting still rage. The streets are choked with bodies and discarded weapons. The Hungarians glance nervously at each other.

Rounding the corner of a small lane, they arrive at a Red Army command post. A long, evil-looking anti-tank gun sits nearby. Communicating with gestures, the Russians direct the Hungarians to haul the gun up towards the sounds of shooting. The Hungarians look around. They have no choice. Gripping the gun by its long trailing arms, they drag it down the road to the corner. The Russians peer around it, then wave urgently for the men to join them. Struggling to heave the anti-tank gun around, my father sees why: Down the lane sits a German tank.

My father is in one of those dream states again, just as when the *shturmovik* charged him a few weeks before. He has survived the most terrifying night of his life, and now he is on the right end of a massive cannon, preparing to aim it at a Nazi tank. His heart pounds hard. But anti-tank guns are meant to be laid in ambush, not dragged out in plain sight of their prey. Standing on top of their vehicle—a massive, heavily armored *Königstiger,* painted in dappled green and brown—the German tankers watch the conscripts attempting to wrestle the heavy gun into the middle of the road. They are elite SS troops in black uniforms. They don't seem particularly concerned. As they clamber down into the turret, my father even sees one or two lazily flick their cigarettes away. A moment later, a burst of flame erupts from the barrel of the tank's gun.

It's the sound that remains with him: like the air is somehow being undone by a searing-hot zipper. Later, my father will surmise the tank gunner fired the shell that was in the breech—an anti-tank round—and probably didn't even bother to aim. Perhaps the loader didn't feel like heaving the thirty-four pound shell back into its rack and repeating the procedure in reverse. Perhaps the gunner, looking through his telescopic sight, saw these were no soldiers but hapless boys.

Whatever the reason, this is what happens. The tank shell, instead of exploding amongst them—perforating them all with fragments of metal, brick, and shards of each others' bones— rockets a few feet over their heads at nearly three times the speed of sound. It strikes the house behind them with a deafening *WHUMP*, punching a perfectly round hole in the wall, the patch still visible during a visit decades later, before continuing out the other side.

The Hungarians scatter like mice. The Russians yell after them but do not shoot. My father, running, throws his military coat to the ground and keeps going. He does not stop until he has reached the villa, where he runs down the basement stairs and rejoins his elated family. He has survived his first and only experience of combat, or something like it.

The Russians will not demand such work of my father again. He is lucky. For some, *málenkij robot* will mean an afternoon of grunt work in exchange for an armful of food. For others, it will be different. Taken because they have German-sounding names, or the wrong-looking face, or simply plucked at random to swell the Soviets' victory tally, perhaps 600,000 Hungarians will be sent to Stalin's labor camps. One in three will die there.

As I stand outside the house in which my family survived its darkest night, or maybe not that house, I feel my gut flipping at the wonder of it: They lived. What were the odds? Later, I'll do the math. In a city then slightly less populous than present-day Dallas, it's as if every single day, for a hundred days in a row, an average of 1,600 people died: Bombed, shot, starved, or killed by disease. Over 80% of Budapest's structures are damaged or outright destroyed. And yet all four of my immediate family—Muki, Csurka, Csupi and my father—survived both the Holocaust and one of the worst urban battles in history.

But the Russians aren't finished with them yet.

56

Budapest, February 1945: The Russians return. Other Russians, searching for provisions, or anything else of value.

They tramp downstairs, into the cellar. They size up my grand-mother and my aunt. They are drunk.

A look passes between Csurka and Csupi. Csurka, unblink-ing, turns calmly to my father. "Gyuri," she says. "Go fetch some kindling."

A black curtain descending over his vision, my father walks up the wooden stairs to the outside. The Russians set down their guns.

As one of the men leads her to a corner of the basement, Csurka turns to her daughter and says, very quietly: "Just think that a passing bird has soiled you."

It was Csupi herself who'd told me this, earlier on the phone. "My mother was such an angel, but unsexed. She never felt any-thing for sex. She told me afterwards 'You are not dirtied, noth-ing happened to you.' We were lucky, we did not become sick. It only happened once. One Russian is enough for a lifetime."

But I already knew this. My father told me this once when I was still quite young, a strange tone to his voice as though he were very gently being choked. And of course Csurka told me herself, in her way: With her stony silence, the way she carried herself like the black sun at the heart of our family's solar system.

I start back down Fillér Street towards the city, my aunt's words still ringing in my ears. "When we emerged from the basement, we had to step over bodies like crumpled paper," she said. "Everywhere, so many young people. At the bottom of the hill was a Russian soldier slumped against a wall, dead. He was very young, short, with pale hair and a fine jaw. There was a red blush to his cheeks. This is what I will never forget: The smile on his face."

But as I walk back down the hill, it's my father's image that haunts me. The good and dutiful son, the helper. By dint of his wits and his pluck he'd lived, saved his own father's life, survived a brush with a German tank. And yet still he'd felt the need to embellish his story, to create projections nowhere near as stirring as the simple truth.

I understand now that I'll never really know when and where this compulsion began, the need to create an idealized version of how things ought to have been. But if I had to guess, it'd be here. My father would go on to live an eventful life, fathering children, forging a successful career. But for all he'd done and all he'd survived, he hadn't managed to save his mother and his sister, the ones he was supposed to protect. Face to face with drunken men with sub-machine guns, he felt, somehow, as though it were all his fault.

Csupi's words came back to me now, expressing a compassion towards the men who'd raped her and her mother that shocked me with its tenderness. "They were mad for drink," she said. "Simple people, peasants, all drunk. They had to be, to get through what they were doing." She paused for a moment. "When the snow finally melted, two weeks later, the smell was unimaginable."

My aunt's words pierced me. Finally, I had an idea of what my family had survived, and what their ordeal had taken from them. And yet enfolded in her words was a simple acceptance, one that my father had never been able to generate towards himself.

57

Budapest, June 2019: It's been days since I've spoken with Julianna, and something's changed. Much as I've relied on her this trip, much as I crave the sound of her kind voice, I've gone someplace she can't: Deep into the cavern of my family's ancestral memories, and also my own. The last few days have ushered me through some portal, and I sense that I'm finally ready for the confrontation I came here for.

When he's not at his farmhouse, Pal and I take evening strolls through his neighborhood. It's during one of these rambles that he takes me to an anonymous little cellar bar. The ceilings are low, the patrons few. The walls are adorned with random images: Old postcards, a painting of Nick Cave, clippings from vintage art books. Amidst the Hungarian folk ballads I hear vintage ska, the Russian rave-punk of Little Big, even a message from home: The loping dub of Joe Lally's intro to "Waiting Room." I love the place at first sight, and I often come for a nightcap before settling into yet another sleepless night on the couch.

One evening, a couple of days after my trip to Fillér Street, I descend the stone staircase to the bar and hear a familiar sound. It's Bauhaus' "Bela Lugosi's Dead" slithering from the tinny speakers. Just that evening I'd perched on the tiny balcony outside Pal's flat, watching bats wheel and dive through invisible clouds of insects. *Is Bela Lugosi truly dead?* I idly wondered. The stage was set for some sort of vampiric ritual.

Pal is in Lókút again, so I sit by myself and sip my beer, admiring the way the tape delay on Daniel Ash's guitar pings off the ancient masonry. I'm reminded of the underground complexes in Lascaux, where the epochal cave paintings—prehistoric aurochs, horses, and stags—were created only where the dimensions of the galleries had a certain resonance. It was the painters' ears, not their eyes, that led them to the right place. Now it's sound that's pulling me deeper as well: The quiet slosh of the Danube, the murmurs of Hungarian voices, they're all begging my attention. I'm still not sure what I was brought here to do, to leave behind or take home with me. But some nascent part of me knows. Here, in this timeless city, it's time to stop believing my life has all been some cosmic mistake.

It's on the walk back to Pal's flat that I feel the first tickle in my belly. Did I eat something I shouldn't have? I can't think where or when. In the distance I hear the mournful whistle of a train departing Nyugati Station. I quicken my pace. I key open the heavy gate, ride the rickety elevator upwards and prepare for bed. My unease is growing, my stomach churning as it does in that pregnant hour between the first draught of ayahuasca and the medicine's full envelopment. I lie down, plug in my headphones and fall fitfully into music: The breakneck thrash of Hüsker Dü, coruscating sheets of feedback dripping down dank basement walls. The music is a rope knotted around my wrist, pulling me down, deeper and deeper.

Now I feel the dread of this long-delayed confrontation with myself. My skin feels clammy; waves of nausea roll through me. I feel frightened. But flashing through the miasma are tiny glimmers. These last weeks the stories of my failure have disintegrated, antique tape loops crumbling into flakes of cellulose. *I was called here, and this was never supposed to be easy.* I remember those nights of childhood earaches so many years ago, the sense I'd been infected by a silent spell. A faint knowing begins to bloom as I writhe against the wrenching in my gut and the pounding in my head: The train has returned. *Mutasd meg nekem.* Show me. I am ready.

Outside I hear distant sirens, the occasional closing of a door somewhere below. Unseen doors open and close inside me as well, taking me back to that afternoon in my parents' bedroom.

58

Washington D.C., Tuesday, September 16, 1975: The house is quiet; Stacey and Csurka are downstairs. I'm sitting on one of the two upholstered benches at the foot of my parents' bed. Everything around me is of a matching pair. The benches; the sleek Danish-made dressers of oiled wood; the modish lounge chairs. Two of everything, about to become one.

I hear the garage door open and close: My father is finally home. He walks quietly up the seven stairs to the landing, then three more and through the door. Into the bedroom, past the his-and-hers walk-in closets flanking the entrance. He enters the room, but he doesn't meet my gaze. He's crying.

Gently, softly, with no rending of wood or brick, the room detaches itself from the house and rises free. Looking out the picture window, I see the backyard receding below me as the bedroom, freed from its rightful place, ascends into the silent nothingness of space. My father still does not meet my gaze. Does he say, simply, "She's gone," or do I imagine it? Painlessly, with an almost imperceptible tug, my tether to the world outside snaps forever. I understand with adult clarity that I'm supposed to cry now too. And so I do, the first and perhaps only time I'm able to summon my tears on command.

I can take it; I will be strong for you.

Some enchantment enters me now, a dark flock settling upon a moonlit roof. I want nothing but to take my father's sadness away. The ambient haloes of pain seek a new host, and I—all of four years old and not knowing what I'm agreeing to—say *yes.* This is the moment where the vivid Kodachrome of those home movies ends. From here on out, everything will be in black and white.

Now the scene toggles back to Budapest, where the almost fifty-year-old me writhes on the threadbare couch. I've revisited this memory many times, the origin story of my own accursedness. But something is different. It's as if the reel of film has slowed down, and I see now what I couldn't before: my father's guilt. He thinks it's his fault, that it's his self-protectiveness and elusiveness that have killed my mother. That he's done it wrong, just like in the basement on Fillér Street. Behind him stands a shadowy figure: It's my grandmother Csurka, hunched in a hand-knitted shawl. She's whispering in his ear, but I understand perfectly what she's saying: *Let him take it. He is her son, after all. You are too precious; I cannot bear to see you suffer any more.*

My father's movie intermingles with mine and now the films are jammed, the acetate smoldering under the searing lamplight. I can't tell what's true anymore; is it his guilt I feel, or my own? A therapist once told me that children often blame themselves for the death of a parent. It's only now that I finally grasp its truth.

A few months before, I'd taken a week-long writing retreat at the Oregon coast. One afternoon, during my monthly phone call with Deborah, the conversation drifted to the topic of Rhonda. "It's like this void," I said, "a space where there's supposed to be memories, but there aren't. I barely remember her. She looks so different in all the photos, sometimes it's like I don't even know what she looked like."

"Oh, sweetheart," she said. "I can tell you this much: Rhonda was at her best when she was with you. There were no hard edges. She was your soul mate."

I stood at the window and gazed out across the Columbia River. In the next yard, a young couple played with their toddler on a grassy lawn. Early-Spring sunlight shone down on the three of them, and in that moment I felt something coming gently undone inside, my sadness floating up like a balloon into the edgeless blue sky. I couldn't change what'd happened, but my mother was still somewhere inside me. If I wanted to find her, all I had to do was look.

Now, on Pal's couch, the scene in my parents' bedroom repeats in endless loop. We were all of us children forced to be adults too soon: Muki, Csurka, my father, Csupi, Deborah, me. I turn to the child inside and enfold him in my arms. *I'm still here; I didn't go anywhere.* He doesn't say a word, but I feel him collapsing into me. Despite the sorrow and the pain ripping through my guts, I feel a blessed wholeness and peace. There is no mistake, no doing it wrong. Everything—even the wracking grief of losing my soul mate so young—is all right. It just is.

A gentle hand pushes down on my chest, and I know what I must do. Fumbling in the side pocket of my rucksack, I find the piece of translucent quartz the woman at that final ayahuasca ceremony gave me. I've never really held it before, felt its weight in my hand. Now I clutch it tightly, noting the way my thumb fits perfectly to its crown. Spurred by the waves of nausea, I turn to face my father and my grandmother and I ask them—*kindly, gently, firmly*—to take it back. To release the spell that allowed me to absorb their pain, to be the family's designated feeler and warehouse of emotion. To take back everything I'd agreed to, and place it instead in this chunk of stone.

I have no idea how long I hold the piece of quartz, willing the poison in me to leave. But eventually I know it's gone. I carefully wrap the stone in paper and place it back in my rucksack. Then I collapse into the sleep of the dead.

59

Budapest, June 2019: All told I'll spend three days in this sickness. When the headaches and cramps roil through me like thunderheads, I'm more or less immobile. I close my eyes and open my ears instead. The soundtrack switches from vintage punk to the dark magnetism of Johannes Brahms's cello sonatas, sinuous spirals incising themselves on ancient tablets of stone.

That first night, unbeknownst to me, the river claimed its latest victims. After I finally fell asleep, two tour boats collided under the eastern span of the Margit Bridge, only a few hundred feet away from me. The smaller one sank in seven seconds, killing twenty-seven.

Once a day I leave the apartment for fresh air and a change of scene, but the streets feel as unloving as ever. Hard-eyed men and women cough, smoke, and glare. At tram stops, stooped elderly people fish items out of trash bins. Again and again I walk by gaggles of tourists, the guides all reading from the same script: "*And then, in 1944, the fascists did _______, and _______.*" I find myself furious, wanting to scream at them: "*You* were the fascists! No one forced you to kill the Jews! *You* killed them, *you* took their belongings, and you won't even own it!"

I hold my tongue.

A couple of days later, Pal drives me to a quiet village on the Danube. After he parks at a small boat launch, I get out to stand on the bank and take in a scene of inspiring grace. We're upstream from Budapest and the river is wider here, a great semicircle cutting through ancient forest. Fog wreathes a line of distant hills; the calls of waterfowl echo off the still waters. It's a vista my father would have loved. He probably stood at this spot himself, many years ago.

A gentle drizzle bathes me, and I reflect on my father's double life here. When I'd sat with Antal and Aliz the week before, I remarked that when I was a teenager, my father would browbeat me into waxing his car. Antal's eyes widened: "You know he brought this, what you call it, *paste* for me to use on my car?" I laughed out loud: George Lorinczi, jet-setting attorney, bringing Turtle Wax all the way to Hungary, just so he'd have someone to detail a car with. In America, my father had everything: a family, a successful career, an active social life. Why did he return again and again to the country that'd so roundly rejected him? Standing here on the riverbank, I finally have an inkling. Unlike the mouth of the Potomac where he and I used to cruise, the waters here aren't brackish. Here in Hungary, he knew exactly where he stood.

This entire trip, I've felt like I was chasing my father's ghost. Now, by the quiet waters of the Danube, I finally sense his presence. He led me here, right to this very spot, the threads of his story dangling in plain sight. From somewhere very far away, I feel the faintest of tremors in the damp air. My father was never the type to let down his guard or express the depths of his sadness. But I sense, just for an instant, that he's finally taken off his mask.

I see you, Dad.

On the drive back to Budapest we pass a billboard for Hell, the energy drink. Pal grins as we speed by Bruce Willis's gigantic image: "Do you know the company had to pay him so much they almost went bankrupt?" Just imagining what Hell tastes like makes me feel queasy again.

I have one final errand to perform. Two days later, Pal having driven ahead to Lókút, I take a cross-country train out to meet him. The station in Győr is ominous and decrepit. As I search for my cousin, hollow-eyed boys with dirty faces approach to mumble at me. I'm grateful when Pal arrives in his trusty cargo van, Lili the wolfhound wedged among the tools and blankets in the back.

On the drive out to the village the roads become smaller and dustier. Pal indulgently pulls off a two-lane road and points. In the distance, a trio of slender jackrabbits caper about the rows. Nearby, two roe deer—small, graceful creatures like miniature antelope—bound away from us with breathtaking poise.

Pal's farmhouse is a dream. A low-roofed building built nearly 150 years ago, it enfolds me in doorways of arched stone. The walls are thick and timeless, built for people whose days began with the lighting of a fire, a groggy glance to the heavens to gauge the weather. Outside, the walled garden throngs with fruit trees around an ancient well. To the north, the property looks out into a lush and rampant field, the last light of the day daubing the grass in liquid gold. The air throbs with the sounds of birdcalls and insects. As we stand at the fence, a pheasant startles from the underbrush.

Pal is an excellent cook, and he prepares us a simple feast from the garden: summer squash with sheep's milk cheese, herbs and olive oil; a vegetable lasagna. We sample from his enviable collection of *palinka*: an eight-year-old plum brandy aged in oak, a rawer apple-plum variety, even a purple-hued one from Transylvania, macerated with wild blueberries. Lili nuzzles me until I romp with her in the yard. Above our heads, the uncountable galaxies whirl and turn in the crystalline air. Pal and I could talk for years. He's one of very few people to whom I never have to explain myself, who accepts me at face value. I feel truly, completely at peace.

The next morning, I arise fuzzy-headed with the morning light. As I sip a stovetop espresso, the air rings with expectant twitterings. I strap my rucksack firmly to my back and walk into the field behind Pal's farmhouse. The early-June sun beats down as I wade through tall grass. I don't know where I'm going, other than far away from anyplace anyone will ever think to look. I ford a small stream and find myself in a sparse thicket. There are no human-made structures around, only the trees and a quiet trickle of water.

I check the time. According to the astrology newsletter I subscribe to, the new moon will turn in a couple of minutes. Why this seems important, I don't know. Why anything about the little ritual I'm about to enact seems important, I don't know. I am merely following directions. My heart thumps ever so slightly in my chest.

Taking a borrowed trowel from my bag, I dig a small hole in the underbrush. When the moment of the new moon arrives I pull out the chunk of quartz, still wrapped in its protective paper. Careful not to touch it myself, I place the stone at the bottom of the hole. I thank it for its service as a holder of curses, of misbegotten obligations and ancestral spells. Then I cover it with dark earth, pack it firmly into place, and walk away.

CODA

My mother and I, circa 1973.

60

Portland, July 2022: "I'm so thrilled to welcome you to *Judaism & The Psychedelic Renaissance,* a truly first-of-its-kind live event," says Rabbi Josh. "And to kick the day off, will you please welcome Seth Lorinczi, here to discuss ancestral trauma and his forthcoming book!"

I nod my thanks to Josh and step up to the podium. Before me is a small sea of faces, some of them familiar, most of them not. There's Julianna; she's only just returned from a trip to record her devotional songs, the ones she started around the time I began writing this book. They've coalesced into a stunning album, and you already know its name: *Imaginal Discs.* Next to her sits our daughter, Evelyn. Much to my surprise, she's insisted on coming to hear me speak.

Perhaps I shouldn't be surprised. A year earlier, when she was 13, I'd asked her to take a walk with me in Kelley Point Park, where the Columbia and the Willamette Rivers meet. We meandered down leafy trails, stopping once or twice at the sight of a bobbing white cottontail disappearing into the underbrush.

Finally, I launched into what I'd brought her here for: It was time to join the threads of our lives together.

"So, you've probably noticed how stuff with mom has changed in the last few years," I began. "How different our lives are, and how much better it's been."

She nodded, slightly wary.

"Well, I wanted to explain a little of what's behind that. I know you get a good bit of anti-drug messaging at school, and I wanted you to absorb that this is how much of our culture views psychedelics. But people have always looked for ways to look beyond what they can ordinarily see. Our therapist introduced your mom and I to psychedelics when we were in crisis, and they really helped us. In fact, they changed everything."

"Yeah, I can tell," she said. "It seemed kind of…tense before."

"I know, and I know that must have rubbed off on you. I think you know it was nothing you did, but I want you to hear that from me directly. And I'm sorry, truly."

She nodded again.

"So, you don't have to do anything with this knowledge, but I think you're ready to know that this is an aspect of our lives. You don't have to try them yourself, or not try them, or do anything right now. You're going to have to come to your own conclusions about whether or not they play a role in your life. But know that what the culture tells us isn't the only side of the story."

I recognized, not for the first time, that while Evelyn would be living under our roof for a few more years, she was fully her own person now. And while she had to have absorbed some of the unexamined trauma that had run my life for so long, it wasn't going to rule hers. She had an emotional wisdom and vocabulary that far outstripped mine at her age, and while she didn't sound anxious to try psychedelics herself, her pointed questions—what my experiences shown me, how they'd changed how I saw myself—put me at ease. I knew she had all the tools she needed to come to her own conclusions. I thought back to the first night Julianna and I had stepped through Renee's door and into our lives, and I felt a deep and abiding gratitude.

Now, at the event, it's not quite nervousness I feel. More the sense of standing up on a moving surfboard, something I've never been able to pull off before. *Can I really do this? I guess we're all about to find out.*

"Hi folks, and thank you so much for being here today," I begin. "Before I start, just a quick show of hands. Who started their day with coffee or tea? Microdose? Pre-granola DMT? I just want to know who I'm dealing with here today...."

At the ripple of appreciative chuckles, I feel the first pulses of a wave urging me onwards. "This day has been a long time coming, and I know that my co-organizers Josh, Donna, and I have put together something truly special for you. As you know, psychedelics are already helping thousands of us identify and come to grips with the weight of ancestral trauma. Well, my journey happened to come in the process of writing a book. Here's how it happened."

I spend the next forty minutes sharing a very condensed version of the book you've just read, illustrated with footage taken from those DVDs of home movies and my trip to Budapest. My public speaking chops are rusty after a two-and-a-half years of pandemic living, but no one seems to mind. As I unreel my story, the nodding heads and even occasional bursts of applause—"Yes, MDMA really *did* save my marriage!"—tell me I'm on the right track.

There's not enough time to share everything, of course. One of the things I leave out is that last night in Budapest, three years before. After a celebratory meal, Pal took me aside and in a quietly pained voice explained that many of his friends didn't know he was Jewish. "Could you not write this?" he'd asked.

After the initial shock, I felt infused by a deep sadness. And so, nearly eighty years after the end of the Holocaust, I've altered all the identifying details of my Hungarian family.

After my presentation there's a Q&A. If I'm still unsure how my talk landed, the audience's eager questions put my doubts to rest. It's clear that many of the attendees have struggled with similar traumas and that psychedelics are helping them heal too. I also feel a quiet sense of pride: After all it was I, along with my two collaborators, who made this day happen.

It's time to wind my presentation up and take a final question. Josh hands the microphone to a woman seated near the front. "Thank you for sharing your story," she says. "But did psychedelics really 'cure' you?"

That's a question I've wrestled with myself, and for a moment I pause. I think back on all the stages of this journey. MDMA had opened my heart, ayahuasca had reawakened my vision, and toad had broken me free from an outdated version of myself. And of course, my trip to Hungary was merely another journey, an opportunity to put everything I'd been shown to use.

I knew I'd returned a changed person, but it would take months for me to understand just how. Those sleepless nights I'd spent wrestling with self-doubt had expanded my tolerance for discomfort. Now I found I could metabolize, in small but ever-increasing doses, the old feelings of fear and despair. About the climate disaster we'd sleepwalked our way into, the election of a grossly incompetent serial abuser, the steady backbeat of hate crimes and synagogue shootings. They hadn't shut me down, and I could even smile at the paradox: That things were in fact far worse than I'd allowed myself to see, and yet I was more capable than ever of remaining present. The crucible of my medicine journeys and the trip to Hungary weren't mere navel-gazing; they'd changed me, helped make me the husband, the father, the friend I'd always wanted to be. These thoughts all flash through me as I ponder the woman's question. Finally I answer, my eyes passing over the hushed room.

"Look. Here's what psychedelics *didn't* do: They didn't make me a different person. They didn't erase the anxiety that's written into my very DNA. In fact, in some ways I feel *more* anxious, because I'm allowing a fuller range of feelings than I ever could before.

"But here's the thing: Before psychedelics, I was reading someone else's lines. I wasn't present in my marriage. I wasn't present for my daughter. After them, I went from being someone who hid from his life to someone who's a member of his community. Who's a resource for others who want to wake up, too." I pause to let this sink in. "So yeah, I'm healed. Or…I'm healed enough."

61

Portland, The Present: There's just one more thing I need to tell you about. It happened about a year after I returned from Hungary, when the outlines of my new life were just coming into view.

I awoke at a quarter to six that morning. I'd been dreaming, which wasn't unusual. Most of the time, the details are gone by the time I've levered myself out of bed. But as I made my way to the bathroom on sleep-rubbered legs, the depth of what I'd been shown swam into focus like some great fish rising from the deep. I felt a growing sense that I'd left my nighttime vision only to enter another one, a waking dream that might never end.

It begins at a party, the kind my roommates and I hosted in our twenties. A dark and cluttered apartment, young people in thrift-store chic. The party is breaking up, and as I watch the guests departing I feel a familiar sadness. They've moved on, leaving me with only the empty bottles and cans for company.

The scene repeats: A slightly different party, a slightly different apartment. But now something calls me outside and I find myself walking through dark cobblestoned streets. I'm not alone, though I can't make out my companions' faces. Ahead, a red glow in the sky heralds activity. Whether it's the celebratory glare of fireworks or an ominous eruption of chaos and fire, I can't be sure.

Soon enough I get an answer. Approaching out of the night is a gaunt and grizzled man in dirty dungarees and a trucker cap. He's swinging an angular sword in rigid chopping motions, and I notice his rusting, mechanical penis. He's a Proud Boy, a far-right militiaman. My companions and I are on our guard, but the man's movements are awkward and stiff, his attacks easy to dodge. A few more such men appear on our walk, but we evade them as well.

Now we've arrived at another party, a much grander one. It's in my old neighborhood, the one I grew up in. People of every age roam the streets and lawns, and the trees are festooned with colorful streamers. We arrive in a basement just like the one of the house I grew up in, that great house built into the hill. The room heaves with activity as elegantly dressed partygoers bustle over decorations and trays of fancy foods. And there's my mother, Rhonda.

Though she died forty-five years ago—nearly to the day—my mother has never once appeared in my dreams. Justice Ruth Bader Ginsburg had passed away the day before, and it was difficult to admit the depths of my grief. Between the coming election and Portland's being shrouded in toxic wildfire smoke, my anxiety was running high. Ginsburg was only four years older than my mother; they'd both made women's equality the focus of their careers. I wonder where Rhonda's path would've ended, had she returned to it. Had she lived.

I'm overjoyed to see my mother. Without stopping to think, I spill out the story of my life, telling her everything that's happened since we last saw each other. She seems attentive, a half-smile upon her lips. But she doesn't look up from her work, carefully lighting candles and oil lamps, arranging platters of food.

Now we walk out among the throngs of guests, through the elegant lawns of my childhood. My vision has taken on an unusual cast: The colors are rich and saturated, just like the Kodachrome of those old family films. I realize the party is drawing to a close and there's still so much more to say. But I'm not sad; I know we'll see each other again. It's only when I remember what I've brought with me that I suddenly feel self-conscious. "You know," I say, "I wrote a book about it all...."

Now my mother finally looks up to study my face. In the past, the woman who gave me life seemed to change from photograph to photograph, and it was difficult to know what she even looked like. Now she's no longer a shape-shifter; her features are fixed firmly in place. Her hair is lustrous and thick, just as it was when she died. It will never go grey. My mother beams at me. A full and radiant smile rises through her cheeks to illuminate her eyes. She sighs softly: "I would *love* to read it."

Acknowledgements

Writing a book is hard, especially when you don't know what you're doing. And while it wouldn't be quite accurate to say that I didn't write it by myself—I did, believe me, over and over and over again—I don't know that I would have gotten through it without an immense amount of support. Here's my attempt to acknowledge it, knowing full well that a few words in the back of a book can't possibly do justice to the debt I owe.

First of all, there's my writing group: Omar el-Akkad, Ned Hayes, Beth Adele Long, Ben Parzybok, and Corin Tucker. They read countless revisions, offered reasoned and supremely useful advice, and probably weathered more than a fair bit of hand-wringing and neuroses on my part. When I couldn't see the way ahead, they helped lead me to it with wisdom, patience, and practical advice. Their comradeship is, without exaggeration, a blessing in my life.

Then there are my publishing partners. A few years ago, I was in conversation with Renee the psychedelic therapist—*not her real name, of course*—about how to bring this book into the world. When she asked me what self-publishing it would feel like, my surprisingly immediate reaction was: "Suicide."

I don't say that to disparage self-publishers. Rather, it's a reflection of my own hunger for validation, for the stamp of approval from some Higher Authority (an agent, a publisher, a whatever). So when Beth Adele Long, my aforementioned writing partner, suggested forming a publishing collective, I knew my goose was cooked. After all, I'd just written a book about turning to face my deepest fears. If I couldn't embody that in real life, well…I'd look a bit of a chicken, don't you think? Hence Spiral Path Collective, a very freeform experiment in collective publishing.

Our principals are Julianna Bright, Beth Adele Long, and myself. The mechanics of releasing a book into the world are just as daunting as writing it, but in maddeningly different ways. Having compassionate and trusted colleagues to call upon is a huge deal, and time and again it's validated my decision to pursue this unusual approach towards publishing.

Now's a good time to acknowledge the Regional Arts and Culture Council, better known as RACC. Their generous grants to artists and organizations have helped kickstart countless local creators, myself included. The one I was awarded in 2022 was a crucial vote of confidence in this project, and I'm indebted to the organization and their work.

Then there are the early readers who helped me refine what I was doing: Miyun Park, my sister Stacey Lorinczi, my partner in many endeavors Nathan Reimer, my oldest friend Tim Green, and his father Ted Green. I'm grateful to each of them in different ways, not only for their encouragement but for revealing my own assumptions and biases. Over and above this, very special thanks to Beth Adele Long—who saw what this book could be before I did—and to Cooper Lee Bombardier, who so graciously served as a resource and guide. In addition,

Beth and her partner—the delightfully named (and legitimately delightful) Blake Beanblossom—were both invaluable early readers and proofers.

I will forever be grateful to the Portland author Paul Levy. Over the time I've known him, his audience and reach have expanded exponentially, and with good reason. He's bringing a crucial perspective to the major question of our time: How do we identify and engage with the forces that are actively bringing about humankind's collapse? And yet with all the increased demands on Paul's time and energy, he's never once failed to be an encourager, a resource, and a sounding board. I'm honored—and humbled—to call him a friend.

Then there are the editors who helped guide this book to completion: Justin Hocking, whose beautiful memoir—*The Great Floodgates of the Wonderworld*—served as a beacon for my own work; Frances Badalamenti, who's frustratingly wise and sharp-eyed; and Matthew Sharpe, who provided clear and unstinting feedback just when I needed it most. On a related note, I'd like to thank Richard Nash, who's taught me much. A quiet legend in the publishing world, Richard and his ebullience helped give me hope there was a path for my book to find its way into the world.

A huge thank you to my friends and family in Hungary who not only made my trip possible, but put up with a multitude of repetitive and no doubt irritating questions about our family as well as Hungarian history, language, culture, and food. As challenging as my visit to Hungary was, they made it incalculably more meaningful.

What about all the psychedelic guides and facilitators who appear in this book? I can't name them here, of course, but I'll forever be grateful. The landscape around such work is changing—in ways both positive and negative. All of the people I reference here took serious and consequential risks to share the healing potential of these medicines with me, and I'll eternally be grateful.

Finally, there's my Portland family: My daughter Evelyn and my wife, Julianna Bright. Challenging as this book was for me to complete, I know that it was at times hard on them, too. Evelyn's curiosity and open-heartedness were huge encouragements to me, and her wisdom and resilience give me hope. And as for Julianna, well…uncomfortable as I'm sure it was to be the one of the subjects of this book, she was never unkind or ungenerous. Honest, clear-eyed, and above all loving, she is the reason this book—and the full and connective life I now enjoy—are possible. Words can't express the depths of my gratitude. I love you forever.

Want to support this book? For better or worse, online reviews are a very big deal in helping creative works get discovered. If you enjoyed this book, please consider leaving a review on Amazon, Goodreads, StoryGraph, or the platform of your choice. I'd be grateful.

About the Author

 Seth Lorinczi's writing has appeared in *The Guardian*, *S.F. Chronicle*, and *Maggot Brain*, among other publications and anthologies. He's presented on psychedelics and ancestral trauma at Yale University and the Oregon Jewish Museum, among other venues, and was a co-founder of "Judaism & The Psychedelic Renaissance," a first-of-its-kind live event.

Death Trip is Lorinczi's first book. Previously, excerpts were published in *DoubleBlind*, *Portland Monthly*, *Liminal Journal*, and *Eclectica*. He lives in Portland, OR with his family and their two derpy dogs.